Lying Minds

David Horry

Lying Minds: June 2020

Contents

I count him braver who overcomes his desires than him who conquers his enemies; for the hardest victory is over self.

Aristotle

Introduction

The fight against alcoholism is not the one it seems. We are not fighting the bottle we are fighting our own minds and our minds lie to us. We don't wilfully make poor decisions regarding alcohol; we lack the normal means to make good ones.

Alcoholism is widely held to be a failing of the individual. The general view of society is that alcoholism is a personal weakness and that alcoholics should exercise better control over themselves. But those of us that struggle with alcohol are also completely confused about this apparent lack of control. We make perfectly rational decisions in other aspects of our lives yet despite our most earnest intentions we drink more than we set out to, we drink more often than we mean to, and we drink at the wrong times. It doesn't matter how hard we try we simply cannot control how much we drink... and right there is the misconception: "control". Normal drinkers assume that everyone has the same ability as them to choose whether or not to drink and they judge alcoholics by that standard. But control is not poorly applied by alcoholics, it is predominantly absent. The mental processes responsible for our decision-making regarding alcohol are not functioning normally.

The brain has some automatic mental processes which evolved to improve our chances of survival. We have no awareness of their operating but they direct how we behave under set circumstances and this direction asserts priority over our free will. These processes encourage us to do things that are beneficial to our survival and discourage us from doing things that are harmful. Collectively they are known as the "reward system" and this system normally directs us to act in ways that are helpful, but it operates incorrectly in alcoholics. In us the reward system becomes incorrectly and excessively bound to the acquisition of alcohol and this has terrible consequences.

The reward system works by using feelings to motivate us to behave in certain ways. It encourages us to approach and partake of things that have been good for us previously and it encourages us to move away from things that have been previously found to be dangerous or harmful. The feelings that encourage us to approach are a longing for or wanting and the feelings that encourage us to move away are dislike, disgust or fear.

2

If we act in accordance with the attractive or repulsive feeling then we are released from the motivating urge.

All animals have this reward system and the behaviour of birds at a bird feeder provides a good illustration of how it works. When a bird first takes food at a feeder it does so cautiously but it finds good and plentiful food there and its reward system records this. It remembers the details of the circumstances and it sets up a motivation and a reward for the next time this circumstance is found. The next time the bird sees a similar feeder it is urged to go there by a longing sensation and on feeding there it is rewarded with a feeling of relief from that longing. But the reward system doesn't just encourage repeating behaviour that was previously found to be beneficial, it alters the urgency of taking this action depending on how often it has been successful in the past. If the bird feeder is always well stocked then the bird's visit will always yield food and the reward system recognises that this source is more valuable than others. At each successful visit the reward system increases the importance of visiting this particular feeder. It does this by increasing the intensity of the urge to approach and this increases the intensity of the sense of relief the bird gets on feeding there. But if another bird feeder only occasionally yields food then the intensity of the urge to visit *that* feeder remains small. Any time the bird is in the vicinity of the well-stocked feeder it is encouraged to go and feed there by a strong yearning and every time this feeder is visited and food is taken then the reward system increases the urgency of feeding there again. If that feeder remains reliably stocked then the urgency of going to *that* particular food source becomes more potent than the urge to go to any other, and the bird ends up feeding there almost exclusively.

None of this behaviour involves any thoughtful process. The bird's actions are driven by processes in its brain that are learned, modified and executed entirely automatically. The bird ends up feeding at this feeder almost exclusively but it doesn't make an active decision to do so; it is directed to feed there by mental processes that operate beneath its awareness. The bird doesn't *decide* to feed there, and the bird isn't aware of *why* it goes there, but it feeds there nonetheless. But the reward system that such does a wonderful job of directing beneficial behaviour in the natural world is tricked into behaving incorrectly by alcohol and other drugs.

When we first drink we enjoy the experience; alcohol makes us feel happy and we have a good time. But that happiness is caused by alcohol directly elevating our mood, it isn't caused by our actual circumstances, and this is how the reward system gets tricked. Our reward system responds to a happy circumstance regardless of the fact that it is chemically induced. This makes it record; "that was good, do it again!" And just like the bird at the bird feeder our reward system sets up a motivating urge ready for the next time that alcohol is nearby. The next time we are close to alcohol we are drawn to it by a motivating urge and if we drink we are rewarded with a sensation of relief. If we repeat and repeat this cycle then the motivating urge increases in intensity to become a craving and the reward is the "aaahhh!" of relief we experience on taking the first drink of the day. If this was the whole extent of the reward system then the urge to drink would become more and more powerful every time we drank. Eventually that urge would become so intense that it would overwhelm all other desires or interests and this is precisely what happens to alcoholics. But another facet of the reward system prevents this happening to the great majority of the population.

Just as the reward system encourages us to do things that are beneficial it also discourages us from doing things that are harmful, and drinking is not always an enjoyable or beneficial experience. If we drink too much we get hangovers and drinking too much or drinking at the wrong time can bring unwanted consequences. For most people the reward system is sensitive to these bad outcomes as well as the good ones and in these people it creates motivating urges that *deter* drinking: their reward system doesn't always encourage them to drink, sometimes it opposes it. For most people the reward system includes both encouragements and discouragements with regard to alcohol and their brain automatically urges the appropriate behaviour for a given situation. But there are some people that only build these alcohol-deterring motivations very weakly. About 5% of the population has a reward system that recognises the benefits of alcohol far more strongly than any detrimental consequences. The reward system in these people never builds any significant motivation to avoid alcohol; it only ever grows and grows the intensity of the urge to drink. Most people have an "off" switch for alcohol, but we don't; ours never forms. In us the wordless compulsion to seek out and consume alcohol grows in strength and it grows without limit, far exceeding the normal intensities found in the natural world. Each time we are urged to drink and do so then the reward system increases the importance of doing so even further. This leads to us drinking more and drinking more often, and the urge to drink strengthens without end. But in us the urges to *avoid* drink never gain strength at all. This causes our reward system to enter a runaway state with regard to alcohol. The act of drinking increases the urgency of wanting a drink and this keeps increasing and increasing. But alcoholism is more than excessive drinking caused by a reward system that is locked into an ever-intensifying feedback loop. Other problems emerge as the seriousness of the condition progresses: we change physically, our memory becomes biased, and we change emotionally.

Once we drink regularly and heavily then our body and brain adapt to offset the regular impairment that alcohol causes. One of the noticeable bodily changes is that our heart speeds up and we feel on-edge, ready to respond, as though we are anticipating some sort of imminent danger. But it is the changes in our minds that have the greater impact on us. Our memory becomes heavily biased in favour of remembering drinking as a good experience; positive memories of drinking are reinforced and memories of bad outcomes are diminished. In our memory drinking is always good and the downsides of drinking, while they are remembered, are never remembered as important; they never gain enough significance to act as a deterrent. In our own minds "drinking is good" and we are quite literally unable to recognise the damage that alcohol is actually causing. But not only do our memories become distorted, so too do our emotions. As our brain tries to offset the effects of regular drinking our emotions change in three key ways; we feel a lowered base level of happiness, our social confidence drops, and we feel constantly distressed and irritable. These changes become more pronounced as our addiction strengthens. Now, when we are sober we are gripped by fear, confusion, frustration, despair and a crushing loneliness. But having a drink removes these feelings, so *we now need to drink simply to lift our emotional state to normal.* We are miserable and distressed when we are sober but a drink relieves these feelings and the reward system recognises this. These emotions themselves become drinking triggers and we become urged to drink by the emotional consequences of being sober: fear, distress, confusion, frustration, despair and loneliness. At this point alcohol becomes the medicine that cures the symptoms that are themselves caused by drinking, but drinking more makes these symptoms even worse, so our problem forms into a vicious cycle of deepening hopelessness.

Our insatiable quest for alcohol establishes itself and progresses entirely automatically. We have no idea that our reward system has started to direct our behaviour regarding alcohol and we don't know that this directing motivation is becoming more intense. We aren't even aware that it is operating! Powerful cravings come on us when we encounter circumstances that have yielded alcohol in the past, and powerful cravings come on us when we feel alone, miserable or distressed. We can't stop the cravings from coming, we can't negotiate with them, and we can't ignore them. A normal drinker can choose whether or not to drink and they are prompted to make a choice when they've had enough. But we don't have that freedom of choice because in us that choice is absent; we are never prompted to make it. In us decision to drink has already been made and it has been made in a part of the brain that we can't see into. For us the decision that we *should* drink has already been formed by mental processes that are automatic, involuntary and compelling. Alcoholism is not poor behaviour, but abnormally functioning mental processes. It is not weakness, but an absence of the deterring motivations that would otherwise limit our drinking. In us the idea "I shouldn't drink now" never happens; there is only ever "I should".

When we decide to stop drinking then our mind immediately starts to work against us. Our brain fights our efforts at sobriety because the reward system continues to direct us to drink. In alcoholics the reward system has wound itself up to fever pitch. The motivating urge that directs a bird to a bird feeder is magnified a thousand-fold and compels us to drink. But our intellectual decision to stop drinking has no influence whatsoever on the operation of the reward system. It remains exactly as it was and it still commands us to drink.

Defying the constant and intense compulsion to drink is both difficult and exhausting, but it is not our only challenge; it is only the beginning. We try to mount this herculean effort at a time when our minds have made us depressed, hopeless, afraid and lonely. Our minds scream at us that a drink will make us feel better and the great problem this poses is that it is completely true; a drink really *will* make us feel better, but only briefly; in the longer term a drink makes our predicament even worse. But our minds greatly prefer something now over something later so a drink now holds incredible appeal. Even if we manage to defy the compelling cravings then our minds still do not give up trying to make us drink; they engage a different tactic and start putting the feelings that we should drink into words. Our minds actively create plausible justifications for drinking, and these too must be overcome. Our thoughts run rampant trying to convince us to drink and it seems at times like we are going mad, but we are not. These self-sabotaging mental contortions are as inevitable as cravings and they cannot be avoided. They add an appearance of cunning and deviousness to our addiction and this means that our struggle isn't static; as we close one door it finds another. But recovery from addiction is possible despite how difficult and hopeless it may feel and recovery is possible regardless of how far the condition has progressed. But not only is it possible to stop drinking, it is also *essential*. Alcoholics that do not break free from the downward spiral into hopelessness will die prematurely, usually from organ failure, accident, or suicide.

Alcoholism has been and continues to be studied in depth. A great deal of how the addiction forms, develops and manifests itself is described in intricate detail in thousands of research papers. But these papers describe changes in the body and brain in technical terms and this leaves out something fundamental; it misses how it feels, and feelings are central to our problem. When alcoholics talk to each other about their problem they don't talk about how much they drank or how often, and they don't talk about neurons or hormones or parts of the brain. They talk about how they thought and how they felt. This book explains in plain language how our brain deceives us about alcohol, and the mechanisms that cause that. This is explained through the lens of someone who's been there and has experienced first-hand what it feels like. The information presented here is important because overcoming alcoholism is not the challenge that it seems. Alcohol does not wield some magical power over us. Alcohol does not compel us to drink it, our brain does that. Alcohol does not make us feel persistently depressed, stressed and alone, our brain does that too. And alcohol does not create the lies exhorting us to drink again, our brain does that as well. Addiction uses our own feelings, emotions and intellect against us and we have no direct counter for these. We cannot choose to not feel alone, stressed, anxious or fearful and we can't choose to not feel that primal silent scream that demands that we drink. We also can't choose to *not* have a torrent of self-sabotaging lies churning in our mind, lies that are every bit as cunning, devious and deceitful as we can be. But these sabotaging actions are not illusions or imaginary, they are completely real and we experience them very powerfully. They are real but they are the products of mis-performing mental processes.

Alcoholism is not failure to exercise proper control over our mind, it is that some parts of our mind are purposefully steering us to our own destruction. To completely reverse the direction of these processes is one of the most difficult challenges we will ever meet, but most people struggling with alcohol don't even know that these processes exist let alone how they can be altered. Addiction is a fight we are ill-equipped to win as it wields weapons for which we have no direct counter; we can only fight back with willpower and knowledge... but knowledge can greatly improve our chances. When we know how our mind will act against us then we can identify the falsehoods as they come and recognise what will help us combat them and what will not. Most significantly we can avoid being deceived. Our greatest weapon is to know that our fight is not with the bottle at all, it is with ourselves.

Alcohol and the reward system

Something remarkable happens when we experience a craving for a drink and then take one. We lift the glass to our lips and swallow and then get an immediate sense of ease and comfort; the extraordinary thing about this is that the sensation is *immediate*. It takes several minutes for any alcohol swallowed to be absorbed in the stomach and then carried through the blood to our brain, yet we get the "aaahhh!" sensation immediately... so it can't possibly be alcohol that has causes this, yet the sensation is definitely there. We aren't particularly aware of this but our brain actively *encourages* us to drink by releasing a motivating chemical called "dopamine". Dopamine gives us that wordless and nagging sense of wanting or longing for a drink and when we *do* drink then our brain abruptly stops releasing it; the urging has done its job and is no longer needed. The tension of the nagging insistence suddenly stops and this is what gives us that strong wave of relief we get when we take our first drink.

Our brain is enormously sophisticated but at a cellular level its operation is remarkably simple. Nerve cells, or "neurons" are connected to each other and pass signals from one cell to the next. Each cell is shaped like a tree, with roots at one end, a trunk, and branches at the other. Brains cells connect to each other root-tip to branch tip where there is a tiny gap called a synapse. A signal is passed from one cell to the next when a chemical called a neurotransmitter is ejected from the branch-tip side of one neuron and received on the root-tip side of another. When the neurotransmitter is received then an electrical charge pulses through the trunk to the branch tips of the cell where it causes neurotransmitters to be expelled from the tips to the next cells. The huge complexity of the brain comes from three elements; the brain has roughly a hundred billion brain cells, each neuron is connected on average to seven thousand others, and there are over two hundred different chemicals that work as neurotransmitters. Precisely what signal is propagated through the brain depends not only on the cells that it connects to but also the particular neurotransmitter that is passed. So the number of possible pathways through any given part of the brain is of truly astronomical proportions, and pathways behave differently depending on the neurotransmitter passed.

Proper functioning of the brain requires that neurotransmitters are reliably passed from one neuron to the next and alcohol interferes with this. Once the correct passage of a neurotransmitter is disturbed then this has consequences for all subsequent neurons in the path, so any disruption at all has far-reaching consequences.

The reward system performs several specific tasks within the brain and the neurotransmitter that activates these is dopamine. Whenever we experience something particularly good we feel joy, delight or excitement and the reward system records this. It releases dopamine down one nerve pathway which makes the brain remember the current circumstances and surroundings. This becomes a reference memory and these reference circumstances are known as 'triggers'. The next time the circumstances of the trigger are encountered then dopamine is activated in another pathway and this pathway creates a feeling of wanting or longing-for: a craving. Finally, if we secure the object of the trigger then the dopamine release is suddenly stopped and we experience this as immediate relief. Dopamine is responsible for all of these actions relating to wanting or longing for something but it also has other roles in the brain and significantly it enhances memory fixation. When we drink then alcohol is absorbed into the bloodstream and soon some of that passes through the blood-brain barrier where it artificially causes the release of dopamine and another neurotransmitter called serotonin. When we drink significantly then we feel happy, carefree and sociable but this is not caused by alcohol; this change in mood comes from the serotonin that has been released. But this happiness has another effect. The reward system recognises that we are enjoying ourselves and it creates a trigger for the circumstances: "that was good, do it again" and the elevated dopamine level imprints this message strongly. Whenever we drink a significant amount then this *always* causes dopamine and serotonin to be released, so the reward system creates and then strongly remembers a new trigger every single time we drink a significant amount in a new circumstance.

The triggers of the reward system, once established, remain in place forever. This is a feature of how the brain works: what has become known cannot become unknown. Once a trigger has been formed then it can never be removed and neither can its associated motivating urge. But while the components of a trigger become permanent on formation they are not entirely fixed: the trigger can't be removed but its vigour *can* be changed.

A single fact or detail is stored in the brain in a group of connected neurons. These groups of connected neurons behave in one respect like a muscle in that just as a muscle gets stronger and faster with exercise so does a group of neurons that fire together. Neurons that work in groups like this are called neural pathways and the more often a neural pathway is traversed then the faster and firmer it becomes. New triggers get formed whenever we meet a new circumstance that we enjoy, but if we meet a circumstance that is already a known trigger then the neurons encapsulating that trigger are activated and it becomes stronger and faster: the more often we access a trigger the faster and firmer it becomes. Triggers that are accessed frequently become lightning fast and are found before other triggers related to similar circumstance. But not only does a regularly exercised trigger become quicker it also gains vigour and when it does that it releases more dopamine. The more often we drink in response to a particular trigger then the more powerful the intensity of the craving sensation becomes. But there is something else that makes a trigger function more powerfully, and that is closeness.

Evolution made the reward system impart urgency to doing things that benefit survival. However, something beneficial like a food that is available now might not be found again for some time, so the reward system encourages us to take advantage of the opportunity while it is present; but it also encourages us do so efficiently. If for example there is a bird in the middle of a field of fruiting berry bushes then there are berries all around it. There is good food in every direction but it would be inefficient in terms of energy use for the bird to pick berries randomly from all corners of the field. So the reward system evolved to use energy efficiently by encouraging the bird to take the closest ones first. The motivating urge launched by a trigger is stronger when its subject is closer than when the subject is more distant. In terms of alcohol this means that a craving to drink is far more powerful when we are close to the triggering circumstance. But it also means that if we begin drinking in a location where alcohol is freely available then we experience another craving for a drink as soon as we have finished our first one. Once we have started drinking in a place where alcohol is available then our reward system demands that we continue. This encourages us to drink more and to drink for longer than we intended when we first arrived at the location.

Every new circumstance in which we drink forms a new trigger and our brain constantly scans incoming information looking for triggering circumstances that have been met before. Directly seeing or smelling the subject of a trigger will make that trigger fire, but triggers are by no means limited to this direct identification. A flying bird may not be able to see the actual berries on a bush but it can see that the bush is of a type that bears good fruit. And the bird may be so far away that it can't even see the bush but it can see the terrain that bushes of this type grow. The bird forms triggers for the berries, bushes of the correct form and for the terrain that supports this type of bush and we do exactly the same with alcohol. Yes, we form a trigger to drink whenever we see or smell alcohol but we also form a trigger for a place at which we've drunk previously and we also form triggers for the roads that lead to that place. Over an extended period we accumulate hundreds and hundreds of triggers that urge us to drink. The cravings brought on by these triggers grow stronger each time we act on them and they grow stronger as we draw closer to the trigger's location. But the reward system can be fooled regarding closeness. The reward system evolved before the existence of pictures, photographs, television etc. and it evolved before our human ability to visualise and imagine. To the reward system all of these things are recognised as real. It cannot distinguish between a glass containing alcohol and a picture of a glass containing alcohol; both cause cravings to be launched. Photographs of alcohol and images of people drinking will bring on cravings and even imagining these things will cause the related triggers to fire. We can bring powerful cravings on ourselves by simply daydreaming about drinking.

Whether or not drinking becomes compulsive rather than chosen depends on the vigour that the drinking triggers acquire. The intensity of a craving is determined by how close we are to the circumstances of the trigger and also by the number of times that this trigger has been successful in delivering alcohol. The more often we drink in response to the craving initiated by a trigger then the more powerful that trigger becomes: the next craving we get from it will be stronger. The reward system encourages us to drink more and it encourages us to drink more often, and if this continues then the triggers strengthen without limit and we become addicted. But everybody has this reward system, so how come that everyone that ever has a drink doesn't become alcoholic?

Triggers exist to encourage some behaviours and discourage others, but a single subject can have multiple triggers for different circumstances. For example, we might have two triggers for lemons; we may feel the urge squeeze some lemon juice over fried food, but we would recoil strongly from the suggestion we should eat a whole one. Just like the example of the lemon most people have some triggers that encourage them to drink and other triggers that urge them not to. It is the balance of these competing triggers that (most often) prevents them from drinking unwisely. Normal drinkers have triggers motivating *against* drinking too much and they have triggers motivating against drinking at the wrong times. They have triggers linked to the discomforts of drinking too much; hangovers, vomiting, and loss of control, and they have triggers relating to the unwanted consequences of drinking; failing to meet important obligations, doing things that are regretted or shameful and so on. But these alcohol-avoiding triggers do not form properly in alcoholics and the absence of these commits us to a catastrophic trajectory.

The reward system encourages us to do some things but it discourages us from doing some others and how it handles conflicting triggers is central to how addiction forms. If I stand on a hilltop where I can see a long way and I also overlook a large lake or sea then I will get a strong sense of calm: I have put myself close to plenty of water (vital to our survival), I am above the surroundings (therefore safer from predators) and I can see a long way (also, safer from predators). However, if that same hilltop I stand on is a cliff edge then a different trigger will fire and the others will not. The risk of falling is present, and fear is induced to motivate me to move away. Even though I am still in that elevated position where I can see water and I can see a long way I do not experience any sense of calm; I only experience the fear. This is because the trigger to make me step back from the edge is stronger than the triggers saying "here is good", and when triggers compete then the most powerful one prevails. We don't simply feel the effects of the more powerful trigger above those of the weaker triggers, the motivating urges from those other triggers are completely dismissed. But if competing triggers have similar strength then the triggers that discourage harmful behaviours prevail over triggers promoting beneficial behaviours. The evolutionary origin of this preference is quite simple: it is better to miss even the finest of feasts rather than to risk being caught by a predator. However, the extent to which we prefer triggers discouraging harmful actions over triggers encouraging beneficial actions is not entirely fixed across all society; it varies from individual to individual. Some people place higher importance on the triggers encouraging avoidance of danger than they do on the triggers encouraging beneficial behaviours and these people tend to be more timid. On the other hand those that place less importance on the harm-avoiding triggers tend to be more adventurous. Individuals that prefer risk avoidance assign greater strength to the triggers discouraging potentially harmful behaviours, whereas individuals that are more inquisitive, independent or adventurous assign greater strength to the triggers associated with beneficial outcomes. Most addicts are in this second group. We assign much greater strength to drinking triggers than we do to drink-avoiding triggers and this has a profound effect on our drinking behaviour because when triggers compete in us it is far less likely that a drink-avoiding trigger will *ever* prevail over a drink seeking trigger. But there is another characteristic that can prevent some people from forming alcohol-avoiding triggers at all.

Just as a trigger gains power depending on its closeness a similar thing happens in relation to closeness in time: we are attracted to partaking of something beneficial now rather than coming back for it later. The evolutionary origin of this is obvious: take the food now because it might not still be there when we come back. But what if the reward (or penalty) later would be larger than the reward (or penalty) now? How we behave under this circumstance is famously demonstrated by "the Marshmallow Test":- Put a marshmallow in front of a child, tell them that they can have a second one if they can wait ten minutes without eating the first one, and then leave them alone. Some children will resist the urge to eat the single marshmallow knowing that there will be two later, but some will not. The key attribute demonstrated here is that the children who don't wait the ten minutes devalue the extra benefit of another marshmallow over time far more aggressively than the others. These children favour a result now far more strongly than a result later and people having this internal preference form far fewer alcohol-avoiding triggers than everyone else. The extra benefit is still considered valuable for these people, but if that advantage is significantly in the future then it is disregarded in favour of the immediate opportunity. But it isn't only advantageous things that get discounted over time this way, disadvantageous ones do as well. In terms of drink-avoiding triggers this means that for people greatly preferring something now over something later the later penalty of a hangover is diminished to the point that it isn't significant enough to form an alcohol-avoiding trigger. People that are highly motivated by "now" rather than "later" form far fewer alcohol-avoiding triggers because the adverse consequences, though they may be severe, are most often encountered significantly *after* drinking rather than at the same time or very close to it.

Frequently accessed neural pathways become firmer and faster and over time we increase the power of the triggers that we drink in response to. But if our personal characteristics undervalue the repulsing "don't drink now" triggers then when we come to an occasion where we are triggered to both drink and to avoid drink then the weaker trigger is almost always the drink-avoiding trigger and it is dismissed. When this happens we strengthen the trigger that encourages drinking because it was successful but we also weaken the trigger that discourages drinking because this trigger failed to deliver its objective. People that strongly favour "now" over "later" systematically strengthen drinking triggers while also weakening drink-avoiding triggers. Over time the drink-avoiding triggers become so feeble that they are almost never more potent than a drinking trigger; so motivation from the reward system to avoid drinking only rarely occurs. This bias towards favouring drinking triggers over drink-avoiding triggers becomes more marked as we continue to drink and a similar bias develops in our memory.

One of the changes that occur when we drink is that alcohol artificially increases the release of the neurotransmitters serotonin and dopamine. The elevated serotonin release makes us feel less stressed, lifts our mood and makes us more socially engaged. Dopamine is the principal agent in the formation of triggers and the motivating cravings but it has an additional function: in enhances memory fixation. When both serotonin and dopamine are raised then we feel like we are having a good time *and* we remember having fun more firmly. But enhancing the memories of drinking being an enjoyable experience isn't the only distortion; the opposite happens to memories of occasions when drinking had bad outcomes. Memories associated with negative emotions are forgotten more quickly than those associated with positive emotions; this is known as "Fading Affect Bias". Not only do memories of good times while drinking get amplified, our memories of drinking that had bad outcomes get diminished.

Failing to remember the bad experiences of drinking as strongly as the good experiences means that our recall of alcohol is unfaithful and what we remember is not how it was. When we think of drinking then our first memory is always of good and happy times, never bad ones, and in the same way that our reward system becomes hopelessly biased in favour of drinking then so does our memory. "Drinking is good" and "drinking is fun" become the things we know more confidently than anything else and any memory that drinking is bad is a murmur by comparison.

Normal drinkers build strong triggers and memories relating to bad drinking experiences, but we don't. We don't build many alcohol-deterring triggers, and we only have weak memories of bad experiences. This inability to properly recognise the downsides of drinking means that we are still encouraged to drink when others would refrain. For example alcoholics will drink with complete disregard to the fact that a severe hangover will follow because our reward system does not have the trigger that encourages us to avoid this outcome. We are aware that we are drinking enough to get a hangover, but when this thought arrives (if it arrives at all) it comes only as simple information; it has no accompanying motivating urge to refrain, stop or slow down. We do not have a trigger that prompts "that's enough now" we only have a pale memory that says drinking a lot ends with hangovers. What we *do* feel however is a strong compulsion to have another drink and to have another drink right now.

Not only are we encouraged to drink too much we also drink at inappropriate times like before important meetings, at work, or on other occasions where sobriety is expected. Again, this is because we receive no motivating repulse from doing so. In alcoholics the urge to seek out alcohol is very strong, and the impulse to avoid it is barely, if ever, present. So we are always motivated to drink and we are almost never presented with the motivation to desist. We even drink in ways that contradict our own standards of sensible behaviour, and we do this because in the moment our mind always urges us to drink, it never encourages us to stop. For example, we will drink before driving and picking up children. We know this is an extremely dangerous and foolish thing to do and we would condemn this behaviour in others but in the time that precedes picking up the children our mind presents no objection to drinking. In fact the opposite happens; our mind still encourages us to seek out and secure drink regardless of what we are going to do later. We are rewarded with a large dopamine surge on taking that first drink and once we have begun drinking then our brain never says "stop, that's enough!" but instead insists "there's time for one more".

Our problem with alcohol begins and escalates in the reward system in this sequence:-

We drink alcohol which causes the brain to release dopamine and serotonin. The serotonin makes us enjoy the experience of drinking and a trigger is formed. We create another trigger every time we drink under new circumstances. When we encounter the circumstances of an existing trigger then a craving is launched to encourage us to drink. Triggers strengthen every time we drink in response to the craving which makes the next craving to come from that trigger more powerful. We continue to crave alcohol for as long we remain somewhere where alcohol is nearby. The dopamine released in response to drinking also enhances fixation of the memory that this experience was good. But we do not often form counterbalancing alcohol-avoiding triggers, nor do we often form strong memories of occasions of when drinking was unpleasant, damaging or dangerous. In the absence of triggers and memories that encourage avoidance or moderation we drink more, and we drink more often. As we drink over an extended period we accumulate more and more new triggers and our existing triggers grow in strength. Over time the motivating urge to drink grows without limit until it is both incessant and compelling while the triggers to avoid drink are progressively weakened.

Eventually the compulsion to drink overwhelms all other motivations and desires.

This is the process by which our addiction forms but we have no idea at all that this is happening to us. All of the changes described here occur in the reward system and this is a part of the brain that we can't see into; we have no awareness at all of what is going on in there. We don't know when triggers form or when they are activated and we have no idea of the strength they have gained. Our only awareness is of a sudden, wordless and urgent demand to drink but we have no direct knowledge of why we are experiencing this.

The power of the reward system to direct our behaviour cannot be over-stated. Humans stand apart from the rest of the animal realm because of our higher mental functions. Humans have a highly developed sense of self, a remarkable ability to discover and invent solutions to problems, logical thinking and judgement (the means to weigh the pros and cons of any situation). These higher functions require relevant information to be found, compared, chosen and then brought into our awareness for us to consider and this requires a huge computational effort. But the reward system requires none of this and it operates up to a million times faster than our conscious thinking. Not only is the reward system a lot faster it also operates entirely independently and our higher functions are oblivious to its operation. This means that the reward system motivates us to do something *before* our conscious mind has even recognised that there's anything to respond to. For example, we will have jumped back in shock before we are consciously aware of a snake crawling through the grass. We react through our reward system and we respond through our conscious thinking and reaction *always* comes before a considered response. When a drinking trigger is fired we feel a craving before we are even consciously aware that alcohol may be near; we are quite literally directed to have a drink before we've even thought about it.

The reward system is enormously motivating and for most animals it is the principal mechanism driving their behaviour. A bird does not stop and ponder what it will have for lunch or where, it lacks that ability, yet it feeds successfully throughout its life. The reward system will motivate an animal to behave in ways that protect and prolong its life and it is enormously compelling, and if it weren't then the animal would die younger. Directing behaviour is the entire purpose of the reward system, so of course it is a powerful motivator. But there are two characteristics in particular that can tip the reward system into a runaway condition. These are; greatly favouring the benefit of something over its disadvantages, and greatly favouring something now over something later. People having both of these characteristics are susceptible to addiction, and these characteristics are very familiar to us: we want more, and we want more now. This is quite literally written into our DNA. In us the reward system becomes destructively associated with the acquisition of alcohol, but we don't know this has happened. We also have no idea that over a period of time the forces invoked by the reward system have become incredibly powerful. Our behaviour becomes driven by feelings that are involuntary, insistent and beyond our direct control, and they come before any considered thought. They come first, we can't ignore them, we can't turn them off and we can't negotiate with them. They are impervious to reason and both precede and defy logic. These are the forces that drive our addiction; they are primal, compelling and unrelenting.

A person with a worsening alcohol problem is completely unaware of the changes in their brain relating to finding and consuming alcohol. To us everything about our drinking seems normal... everything that is except the way that others are starting to talk about it. As our addiction progresses we sense no change in ourselves but perceive the problem to be "in the eye of the beholder". This is the truth for us as we genuinely perceive no problem because our mind insists that "alcohol is good!" despite what other people tell us.

The onlooker watching someone become steadily more and more regularly drunk sees a problem, but we see none. This is caused by the different perceptions. The onlooker is seeing us from an untainted viewpoint; their memories and triggers associated with alcohol are balanced. To them too much alcohol is bad. But to us, alcohol is good, and more alcohol is also good... and we are completely baffled as to why other people don't see it the same way.

How alcohol affects us

Alcohol doesn't only disrupt the proper operation of the reward system it also has a detrimental effect on many other parts of the body. The gastric system, liver, kidney and brain are all adversely affected by prolonged and regular contact with alcohol.

Alcohol is transported to the organs in this sequence: It is absorbed into the bloodstream in the stomach and intestines. From there it is carried to the liver, the heart and lungs, and then to the brain and muscles. Then some passes through the liver (again), some through the stomach (again) and some through the kidneys. After passing through all the organs and muscles the blood flows back to the lungs and heart where it gets re-oxygenated and re-circulated.

The alcohol trail begins in the stomach and intestines where it is absorbed into the bloodstream and carried to the liver. The liver's principal function is to clean the blood that comes from the stomach and also clean the depleted blood after that's been through the organs and muscles. It is also responsible for some other important functions including making the glucose that our body uses for energy, and breaking down unwanted chemicals that were absorbed into the blood in the stomach during digestion. The liver recognises alcohol as an unwanted toxin and it attempts to remove it, but it can't be removed by filtering, it has to be broken down chemically. Enzymes are biological molecules which change chemicals from one form to another and they have many roles in the body including digestion and waste removal. There are many different types, each performing a specific chemical change, and it takes three different enzymes to completely break down alcohol. One enzyme changes alcohol into acetaldehyde, another changes acetaldehyde into acetic acid and a third changes acetic acid into carbon dioxide and water. But the body isn't evolved to deal with large amounts of alcohol. Alcohol isn't something that occurs in large volumes in nature and we only have a limited quantity of the enzymes that remove it. So when we drink we ingest alcohol far more quickly than these enzymes can break it down and only a little of the alcohol is converted to acetaldehyde on its first pass through the liver. The remaining alcohol and acetaldehyde are carried in the blood until it passes through the liver again. Alcohol and acetaldehyde are only slowly removed, so if we keep drinking then the amount of both alcohol and acetaldehyde in our bloodstream rises. But acetaldehyde is toxic, and it is the build-up of acetaldehyde in our blood that makes us feel sick and gives us a headache.

If we drink routinely and heavily then our liver adapts to this regular demand by increasing the quantity of the enzymes available to remove alcohol and acetaldehyde. But it never produces enough to break down all of the alcohol and acetaldehyde immediately and blood has to pass through the liver many times before these are removed completely. So as we drink the concentrations of alcohol and acetaldehyde in our blood rise and they only subside after we greatly slow down our drinking or stop. But alcohol must first be turned into the toxic acetaldehyde before it can be reduced to the less toxic acetic acid which means that acetaldehyde removal always lags behind alcohol removal. When we stop drinking our blood/alcohol level will start to fall, but the acetaldehyde concentration will still continue to rise, and this is why we get hangovers *after* drinking, not during. The increased quantity of the enzymes that break down alcohol allows the liver to process it away more quickly and this is beneficial to the body, but this causes two changes to our drinking behaviour. Faster removal of alcohol means we are able to drink more before becoming ill, but because alcohol is being removed from our blood more quickly we need to drink faster and we need to drink more in order to feel the same effect as before, and this is precisely what we do: we drink faster than we first did at first and we drink more.

Blood carrying alcohol and acetaldehyde first leaves the liver passing through the heart, lungs, brain and muscles before returning. But this time the blood is divided between three paths. Some blood goes to the liver where more alcohol and acetaldehyde are processed away, some goes to the stomach where the blood takes on more dissolved foodstuffs, and some goes to the kidneys where waste products are removed and the water content of the blood is regulated; but alcohol interferes with how this last part happens.

The kidneys perform a filtering action on blood, separating the wanted from the unwanted. Blood enters the kidney and the water in it is separated from everything else. Blood is then filtered to separate it from waste and if water is needed to replenish the water content of the blood then it is re-absorbed into the clean blood. The other water is jettisoned as urine, taking the waste from the filters as it exits. Whether or not the kidney puts water back into the blood is determined by the presence of a hormone called "vasopressin" which is released by the pituitary gland in the brain. Hormones are chemicals released by various glands around the body that regulate the activity of organs. They are carried in the bloodstream, so they don't act as quickly as neurotransmitters (which are effectively instantaneous) nor do they fade as quickly; they have to be re-absorbed out of the blood for their action to cease. When the kidneys detect vasopressin in the blood then they release water back into the bloodstream, but when there is no vasopressin present then all water is removed and passed as urine. But alcohol slows the brain down and this slowing down causes the pituitary gland to release less vasopressin. This in turn reduces the amount of water being put back into the blood and this is why we become dehydrated when we drink. Drinking water will not fix this shortfall, this is a myth. The kidneys will not re-absorb water into the blood while the pituitary gland does not release vasopressin, and the pituitary gland will not release vasopressin while there is still a significant amount of alcohol in the brain. This means that any extra water we drink will be passed as urine until our blood/alcohol level approaches normal.

While the effects of alcohol on our liver and kidneys are significant, it is what it does in our brain that causes us most trouble. Alcohol disturbs how the brain works at the most basic of levels: it prevents proper performance of neurotransmitters at the synapses. Glutamate and GABA (short for GammaAminoButyric Acid) are neurotransmitters that control the speed of mental function, and alcohol interferes with how both of these work. Glutamate and GABA work in the brain in a similar way that the accelerator pedal (the gas pedal to North American readers) and the brake pedal work in a car. Glutamate makes the next neuron more likely to fire and is like the accelerator pedal, while GABA makes the next neuron less likely to fire and acts like a brake pedal. But alcohol disrupts the normal detection of both of these neurotransmitters at the neuron on the receiving side of a synapse. Alcohol molecules clog up the point on the neuron that detects glutamate and this prevents a glutamate molecule from ever reaching it. This makes the receiving neuron fail to detect when glutamate is present. Even when glutamate is released from the transmitting neuron it doesn't get detected on the receiving side, so the effectiveness of glutamate is reduced. But while alcohol makes glutamate *less* potent it *increases* the apparent effect of GABA. The alcohol molecule is small and this is what allows it to pass through the blood-brain barrier and reach the brain. But this small size and its shape also allows it to fit into the socket meant for detecting the GABA molecule on the receiving neuron. When this happens then the neuron incorrectly signals that GABA has been detected. These two actions combine to trick neurons into believing that glutamate has not been passed at synapses but that GABA has. In the car analogy this is like lifting your foot from the accelerator pedal while also pressing down on the brake; the speeding up of the brain is decreased and the slowing down of the brain is increased. The result of this is that the whole brain slows down, and the more we drink the more it slows down. When we drink a lot then this slowing down of mental function becomes so pronounced that it begins to have serious yet familiar consequences.

The cerebellum is the part of the brain that controls our muscle movements and if we drink a lot then the whole brain slows down, including the cerebellum. This means that it takes a fraction longer for our brain to make a single muscle contract or expand, but when a lot of things all have to happen together, or as a precise sequence in close succession, then they can fail to happen when they are needed. It is this slowing of our brain that causes slurred speech; there is so much to coordinate in such a short time span that the cerebellum is no longer fast enough to do it all correctly. Similarly, when our brain is slowed down then the cerebellum fails to coordinate all the muscles quickly enough to keep us balanced steadily upright. While these two things can be seen by anyone watching us there is a third consequence that is only apparent to ourselves. A slowing down of processing in this part of the brain causes two of the most obvious signs of intoxication; slurred speech, and loss of balance, but the muscles in the eye are also controlled by the cerebellum. Proper operation of the eyes requires coordinating controlling the direction that each eye faces with the focus of each eye to suit the distance to the object it is looking at. But it also involves another step. Our brain is constantly searching for the most significant items in the current scene and then directing our sight to them. This is an enormously complex task of identification and selection but it needs to coordinate this action with continuously moving the eyes and focusing them. These three things have to occur in very close succession; deciding what to look at, turning each eye to directly look at it, and then focusing each eye. When our brain slows down then the coordination and synchronisation of these three tasks starts to fail. Our focusing fails to keep up with the continual eye movement and if we drink enough then our brain also fails to direct both eyes simultaneously to the same point. It is the slowing effect of alcohol on our brain that causes loss of focus and double vision.

Another familiar consequence of drinking too much is memory loss. Everything that comes in through the senses is stored in short term memory for a few seconds. The hippocampus (the part of the brain responsible for memory formation) examines all this information and compares it with everything that is already known. It rejects the information that is either unimportant or familiar and it commits the new, significant, or potentially useful information to long term memory. But this is a huge processing task and when the hippocampus is slowed down by too much alcohol then it is no longer able to process this information quickly enough to keep up with the incoming content... but the inbound content keeps coming. When the hippocampus gets significantly slowed then it fails to reach a conclusion on whether or not information is worth keeping before it has to move on to the next piece. This means that it skips over some new information that *should* be committed to long term memory and it is not remembered at all. We are still upright, conscious and functioning when this occurs but our memory of what is happening around us is incomplete or even missing completely.

The slowing down of our brain has other consequences too; it decreases inhibition, increases our pain threshold, and decreases sexual performance. It also slows down our conscious thinking which severely slows decision-making and prevents completion of proper judgement. But alcohol causes one more particularly significant change in the brain; it alters how ready we are to respond to danger.

We are evolved to be able to react extremely quickly when confronted by something threatening. The mechanism controlling this is known as the "fight-or-flight response" and it detects the presence of danger and then prepares the brain and body to perform to their maximum potential. To do this the body shuts down non-essential activities as well as operations that can be deferred for a while and it concentrates all resources on being able to run or fight at a moment's notice. Three agents prepare this readiness. A neurotransmitter called noradrenaline (also called norepinephrine) is activated throughout the brain and central nervous system. Noradrenaline increases alertness, promotes vigilance, invigorates the formation and retrieval of memory, and focuses attention; it also increases restlessness and anxiety. At the same time the pituitary gland in the brain directs the adrenal gland to release two hormones; cortisol and adrenaline (adrenaline is also called epinephrine). Cortisol is carried in the blood to receptors in most cells in the body, so it has wide reaching effects, but significantly in this context it wakes us from sleep. The other hormone, adrenaline, increases heart rate and stroke volume, dilates the pupils, constricts the blood vessels close to the skin, and dilates the blood vessels in the major muscles. These three act together to prepare us for rapid response, but the release of all three of these agents is controlled by the flight-or-fight response, and when the brain slows then so does the flight-or-fight response. The amount of cortisol, adrenaline and noradrenaline are all reduced when we drink and this brings a very significant reduction in our physical and mental capability; less cortisol means we become sleepy, less noradrenaline makes us mentally dull, and less adrenaline makes us physically lethargic.

When we stop drinking and our blood/alcohol level starts to fall then the flight-or-fight response becomes more active again. Cortisol and adrenaline return to their normal levels but noradrenaline does not, it rises further to abnormal levels. Acetaldehyde is created as alcohol is broken down, but it acetaldehyde is also a releasing agent for noradrenaline. Noradrenaline activity rises as the flight-or-fight response wakes up and then it far exceeds what is normal as the high acetaldehyde level further stimulates its release. This over-excites our nervous system causing the trembling that we call 'the shakes'. The tremors we get after a heavy drinking session are not caused by any nutritional deficiency, nor are they due to a build-up of toxins from whatever we have drunk. The shakes are caused by our body releasing excessive quantities of noradrenaline in response to the abnormal amount of acetaldehyde in our blood which in turn is produced as our liver processes away alcohol.

Another unwanted outcome from the flight-or-fight response is that sometimes it wakes us in the middle of the night. This is caused by the blood/alcohol level dropping sufficiently for the brain to pick up speed again and the flight-or-fight response reactivates. When this happens then cortisol, noradrenaline and adrenaline are again returned to the bloodstream; the cortisol rouses us from sleep, noradrenalin makes us alert, and adrenalin gives us a racing heart. We struggle to get back to sleep and our mind races while our increased heart rate makes us overheat.

These are the bad effects of alcohol, but alcohol does of course have its up-sides otherwise we would never be interested in it at all. The slowing effect of alcohol in the brain has many unwanted effects but it also causes some that we enjoy. Glutamate speeds up the brain which makes us more agitated or anxious while GABA slows the brain making us calmer. So when the effect of glutamate is reduced and the effect of GABA is increased then our anxiety fades as our brain starts to slow down. But a secondary response to this slowing down causes our brain to release more of two neurotransmitters; serotonin and dopamine. Dopamine has many functions in the brain, and its role in triggers, motivation and memory has already been discussed. Alcohol also indirectly causes extra serotonin to be released, and serotonin too has many functions. Among them are; maintaining a balanced mood, boosting self-confidence, and decreasing worries and concerns. When we drink alcohol it causes extra dopamine and serotonin to be released and the serotonin makes us happier, less anxious, calmer, and it increases our social confidence and social engagement. If we drink enough we will, for example, be quite convinced that we are excellent dancers and dance on a table so that everyone can see how good we are. These mood lifting changes are the positive aspects of alcohol and until we drink regularly and heavily then these are the effects that we will experience: drinking makes us happy, care-free, and socially outgoing.

The effects of alcohol on the body and brain are significant and wide-ranging but they don't all happen at once, there is a sequence they pass through. When we take the first drink, then if this drink is in response to a drinking trigger we will get an immediate surge of ease and comfort wash through us as we experience the dopamine released by the reward system. The alcohol is carried to the stomach where it is absorbed into the bloodstream and passes to our liver which starts to break it down, but it can't all be removed immediately.

Alcohol that isn't initially reduced to acetaldehyde circulates in the blood and as we drink more the blood/alcohol level begins to rise and soon the toxic acetaldehyde level starts rising too. But the rising blood/alcohol level also begins to change the correct recognition of GABA and glutamate and our brain starts to slow down. This slowing causes dopamine and serotonin to be released which makes us feel like we are having a good time and the elevated dopamine makes us remember that. As our brain slows down the pituitary gland produces less of the hormone vasopressin and this makes our kidneys stop re-absorbing water back into the blood. We begin to become de-hydrated but we don't care; we're enjoying ourselves. As we continue to drink then our brain further increases the amount of dopamine and serotonin released making us more cheerful, relaxed, care-free and socially confident, but the mental slowing also begins to significantly affect our alertness and mental function. As we continue to drink everything escalates. We become happier, more care free, and excessively self-confident. Unfortunately though, while we feel wonderful, the adverse consequences are escalating too. Increasing blood/alcohol levels slows the brain even further and reduces activation of the flight-or-fight response. This results in reduced alertness, increased drowsiness, a slowed heart rate, dilation of the surface blood vessels (we get a flushed appearance and perspire) and we begin to lose the ability to focus our attention. Eventually complex tasks like balancing and speech can't be performed quickly enough to be successful, so we begin to slur our words and struggle to maintain balance. Our eyes begin to lose focus and if we drink enough they will fail to work as a coordinated pair and we'll develop double-vision. Proper transfer of useful information from short-term to long-term memory begins to fail, and if we continue to drink then we prevent the brain being from being able to form new memories completely. We struggle to stay awake, but if we still continue to drink then our brain will slow down to the point that we lose consciousness.

At the point we stop drinking then the blood/alcohol level stops increasing after the alcohol already in our stomach has been absorbed, but blood toxicity continues to climb as the alcohol still circulating in our blood is steadily converted to more and more acetaldehyde. When we wake we are dehydrated, but most of the alcohol has by now been converted to acetaldehyde. Lower blood/alcohol levels allow serotonin and dopamine to return to their normal states and we are no longer overly happy or confident; but we are now suffering the effects of dehydration and being poisoned by the acetaldehyde: we are hungover. The high acetaldehyde concentration causes noradrenaline to be released throughout the nervous system at abnormally high rates which makes us tremble. Our liver continues to work at breaking down acetaldehyde and eventually our blood/alcohol level drops sufficiently for the brain to speed up again and the pituitary gland finally instructs our kidneys to resume absorbing water back into the bloodstream. Our hangover fades as the toxic acetaldehyde is removed and our body slowly rehydrates.

This is what happens when we drink heavily, and this is the universal experience; it happens to everyone that drinks a lot. Our body's principal reactions to alcohol are identified here, but these functions are not entirely fixed; we evolved to be able to adapt to changing circumstances. If we begin to drink both regularly and heavily then a significant proportion of our day is spent bodily and mentally compromised. Our brain and body slowly adjust to this in an attempt to counter this regular impairment. But the changes that occur, though their aim is to maintain optimal performance, are ultimately the changes that lock our addiction into place.

Alcohol-tolerance

Alcoholism is not about making poor choices in relation to drinking. People that are addicted to alcohol do not have free choice about how much they drink or how often; our free will is compromised by a reward system that urges us ever more compellingly to drink and never to avoid it. The demand that we drink comes as feelings rather than words and we get those feelings before our conscious mind is even aware that alcohol is close. As we continue to drink then the urge to avoid alcohol weakens as the urge to drink more strengthens and drinking gradually becomes more compulsive than chosen. Addiction begins in the reward system and regular and heavy drinking strengthens the urge to drink while diminishing resistance. As we drink more we spend extended periods of time handicapped by alcohol and our brain tries to correct this in an effort to maintain optimal performance. Alcohol has three main effects on our brain; it slows down the processing speed, it artificially alters our mood, and it reduces our readiness for "flight-or-fight". These three are detected as unwanted behaviour and our brain attempts to correct them. But the changes it makes in order to maintain effectiveness also change how we think and how we feel.

The first issue is the speed at which the brain operates. While we drink our brain is slowed by alcohol and this slowing down lasts for as long as there is alcohol in our bloodstream. If we drink regularly and heavily then this slows our brains for a significant portion of our time and this has the effect of lowering our average brain speed across the whole day. Alcohol causes the brain to detect less glutamate than was released and to detect more GABA than was released and our brain does the opposite to try and correct this. It releases more glutamate (the accelerator pedal) and it releases less GABA (the brake pedal). This corrects the slowing down we experience while we are drinking but our brain applies this correction the whole time and this means that our brain now runs faster than normal when we are sober.

> **Consequence #1:** Once our brain adjusts its speed to compensate for regular drinking then we have a racing mind when we are sober.

The second change relates directly to mood. The reasons we enjoy alcohol are that it soothes anxiety, makes us happier and makes us more socially engaged.

But the extra dopamine and serotonin we get when we drink isn't summoned by the brain, its release is artificially caused by alcohol and our brain recognises this. Our brain detects that it is receiving more dopamine and serotonin than it ordered and it responds by reducing their release as well as reducing sensitivity to them (some of the detector points on neurons get turned off). While the brain makes this adjustment to correct a problem that has been detected it has a significant and unwanted impact on how we feel. Like the adjustment for speed this correction is applied 'across the board'. The influence of both dopamine and serotonin is reduced, and it is not just reduced while we drink, it is reduced the whole time. This makes us feel down when we are not drinking and reduces the lift in mood we experience when we drink.

Consequence #2: Once our brain regulates down the effect of dopamine and serotonin then we become more anxious, less happy, less care-free and less sociable when we are sober.

The third change is to do with the "flight-or-fight" response and involves both neurotransmitters and hormones. Together these control our readiness to respond quickly to danger and when we drink regularly the levels of these are lowered for extended periods (the slowed brain activity also lowers the flight-or-fight response). But having the effectiveness of our flight-or-fight response impaired for extended periods is dangerous, it threatens survival and our brain cannot permit this, so it boosts it up. Like the other adaptations this is a wholesale change; the activity of the flight-or-fight response is increased the whole time. More cortisol, adrenaline and noradrenaline are released, and although this reduces the drowsiness, dullness and lethargy that we experience when we drink it means that the flight-or-fight response is over-active when we are sober.

Consequence #3: When we are sober our brain constantly searches for signs of danger, our heart beats faster, blood is diverted from the skin to the large muscles leaving us with a pale complexion, and feeling edgy and restless.

When we drink regularly over an extended period then our brain adjusts the way it operates to minimise the adverse effects of alcohol. This makes us more alcohol-tolerant: we can drink far more before we become mentally and physically compromised. In this respect the adjustments that our brain makes are successful but this comes at a large cost because when we are sober we are; less happy, more irritable and restless, and we lose social confidence. These changes take years rather than months to develop, but they have a profound effect. We were already victims of a reward system in a runaway state, but the changes to how we feel have consequences that guarantee our entrapment.

Addiction is a "progressive" condition; it always gets worse, never better. But the grip of alcoholism tightens so slowly that we don't notice anything changing. We don't notice that the urges to drink become more powerful and more frequent. We don't notice that we drink more and that we drink more often. But the longer we continue to drink the more severe the condition becomes and we *do* begin to notice it. Yes, we drink more and we drink more often than we mean to, but these cease to be our main concerns. As our alcohol-tolerance progresses then all of the changes that the brain and body make to try and correct the alcohol impairment increase in severity and the emotional consequences of this propel us into deepening anxiety and depression.

Lengthy exposure to alcohol reduces the effect of dopamine and serotonin in the part of our brain that experiences emotion. We become; less happy, lacking social confidence, and more concerned by our troubles. As we continue to drink these emotional changes become more pronounced until we feel miserable, surrounded by problems, and intimidated by social contact. The continued reduction in GABA and the increase in glutamate speeds up mental processing even further which leaves our minds racing and churning over all our problems. Our flight-or-fight response continues to raise adrenaline and noradrenaline levels which cause a faster pulse rate, higher blood pressure and temperature, increased sweating, and loss of appetite. We become anxious, fidgety, and restless as our minds constantly search for the danger for which our body has been prepared. But these elevated levels are normally temporary measures to provide us with a quick boost in times of distress and aren't evolved to be elevated over extended periods. There are side-effects to having a permanently elevated flight-or-fight response and some of these can become quite serious.

Cortisol is a key chemical in the proper regulation of sleep. It controls our transition into and out of the deep-sleep state that is vital for proper brain health, and it also wakes us from sleep. Elevated cortisol levels disturb this pattern making it difficult for us to get to sleep and it prevents us from achieving the deep-sleep state needed for proper rest and recovery. Additionally the gastrointestinal system is very sensitive to cortisol and continuously elevated levels can lead to heartburn, abdominal cramps, diarrhoea, and constipation. Also both adrenaline and cortisol cause the liver to put more glucose (sugar) into the bloodstream, and when their concentration is increased over an extended period then we have a persistently high blood sugar level. This is why heavy drinkers are more likely to suffer from diabetes.

All of these changes in our brain and body bring us down. We feel constantly ill-at-ease, and unhappy. We are socially insecure and shy of contact with other people. We are anxious, our hearts pound, our minds race, and are consumed by our own problems. We can't sleep unless we drink but when we drink enough to induce sleep then we wake again as soon as our blood/alcohol level drops. We never achieve deep sleep, and we live in a constant state of chronic fatigue propped up by the stimulating effects of adrenaline and noradrenaline. But there is something that will quickly remove all of these problems and restore us to normal, and that is alcohol. When we drink then our dopamine and serotonin levels rise again, our brain slows down, and our flight-or-fight response stands down from high alert; cortisol, adrenaline and noradrenaline levels drop. Once we have become alcohol-tolerant then alcohol becomes the medicine that removes the symptoms that alcohol has caused, but drinking more only increases their severity.

All of this has an extremely serious consequence and that is that we now *need to drink in order to feel normal.* The only way that we can now regularise the brain and body is to drink. When we are not drinking we are unhappy, agitated, lonely, restless, anxious and depressed. But all of these symptoms are relieved by drinking. The reward system recognises this and when it does so a serious decline in our mental well-being becomes inevitable.

Our addiction is propelled by the reward system. It built drinking triggers relating to our daily routines; the time of day, where we were, people we were with and so on, and these triggers were strengthened each time we acted on them. But once our mood is changed by our alcohol-tolerance then the reward system takes on a new dimension with regard to alcohol. It recognises that our anxiety is eased by drinking, that our depression is lifted by drinking, that our loneliness is relieved by drinking, that our roaring mind is calmed when we drink, and it creates drinking triggers for all of these. Our reward system keeps adding and strengthening emotion-based triggers and over an extended period our first and immediate reaction to any distress at all is that we are triggered to drink. Tired? -> drink, lonely? -> drink, angry? -> drink, hungry? -> drink, stressed? -> drink, anxious? -> drink. All of these emotional states acquire drinking triggers and we constantly crave alcohol when we are not drinking. Being continuously triggered to drink also means that alcohol is constantly brought to the forefront of our mind. Any time we are not drinking then we are thinking about it and even our waking thoughts are of alcohol; when we will get some and where. As we wake from a drinking session our blood/alcohol level is in decline. We may still be hung-over but as soon as the blood/alcohol level drops significantly then all the problems caused by alcohol-tolerance return. As we come around we start to feel agitated by the excessive noradrenaline activity and our reward system responds with a craving. As we move on with the day we become lonely, frustrated, and anxious and all of these bring on cravings. We think about alcohol the whole time we are not drinking and this too launches cravings. Once we become alcohol-tolerant then our position is dire: we become triggered to drink by the emotional consequences of being sober.

At the other end of the day we have to drink to be able to sleep. If we go to bed sober then our flight-or-fight response is so elevated that our minds race, our heart beats fast, we overheat, and the elevated cortisol level expressly prevents sleep. If we want to sleep then we must drink first.

The times of day that we drink are extended, we drink to excess far more frequently, and our alcohol-tolerance adaptations become even more pronounced. Our minds race while we are not drinking, churning over and over all our problems. We become increasingly anxious and depressed and are intimidated by social contact. We are agitated and restless and have a persistent sense of impending doom. We rationalise that we are drinking because our lives are difficult, or stressful, or unsatisfying, but in reality most of the reason we are drinking is because our brain responds to these stresses and demands that we do. We are not drinking in response to our personal circumstances but because our brain is directing us to do so, *but we don't know this*. What we *do* know is that we are drinking a lot but we are oblivious to the extent to which our brain is automatically driving this. Over time the emotional consequences of alcohol-tolerance become so severe that it is impossible to drink enough to overcome them and alcoholics often report that "alcohol stopped working for me". It becomes impossible for us to drink enough to become happy. It doesn't matter how much we drink we can no longer achieve the care-free happiness we once did... we become so insensitive to serotonin and dopamine that this is no longer possible. What initially made us happy now locks us in inescapable hopelessness and the most we can achieve is a partial and temporary relief from it, but that relief only worsens our position in the longer term.

Our addiction begins with an unbalanced reward system that encourages us to drink more often than it encourages us to avoid it. We accumulate many powerful drinking triggers and very few drink-avoiding triggers. This is the principal driver of our addiction but it is alcohol-tolerance that locks it into place. Alcohol-tolerance leaves us with negative emotions whenever we are sober. Drinking relieves these emotions and we develop powerful drinking triggers for them. When we first began drinking our triggers were related to people, places, events, and times of the day, but the negative emotions of alcohol-tolerance now trigger cravings whenever we are sober. Once we have become alcohol-tolerant then the demand to find alcohol becomes continuous so we drink more and this further strengthens triggers and deepens the emotional consequences of drinking. It is a self-reinforcing spiral down into despair.

None of this escalation from having a few drinks a long time ago to becoming completely driven by alcohol is chosen. The whole process happens without our permission, involvement or awareness. We have no idea that the problem has formed, we have no idea the problem is escalating, and by the time we suspect we actually have a problem it is too late; we are already completely trapped.

The psychological burden of addiction

Alcohol tips the reward system into a runaway state that constantly increases the intensity of the compulsion to drink, our memory becomes biased to favour drinking, then our brain adapts to offset the impairment caused by regular drinking and this changes our mood. These are the direct ways that alcohol affects our body and brain. But this book is not about alcohol, it is about alcohol-*ism* and alcoholism isn't just a set of hidden mental processes and chemical changes in the brain, it has psychological consequences too: alcoholism radically alters how we feel about ourselves and our place in the world.

Holding two beliefs that contradict each other causes an inner distress known as "cognitive dissonance". Our minds need information to be resolved and orderly because lack of certainty in the wild can be fatal, so when we have two contradictory pieces of information then our mind tries to remove one or other of the conflicting ideas. The way our mind deals with unresolved information is to bring it to the forefront for further consideration; worry isn't some haphazard occurrence, it is our mind trying to clarify unsatisfactory information. When we worry about something then all related information is compared to the problem to try and resolve it, but when it comes to alcohol our mind tries to reconcile the irreconcilable. The inner distress comes from the contradictory ideas "drinking is good" and "drinking is bad". Both are completely verifiable but they can't possibly both be true. Information supporting "drinking is bad" is real and demonstrable; people tell us (directly or indirectly) that our drinking isn't normal, and we know ourselves that what they say has some truth to it. We also know within ourselves that our drinking is causing us to do things we wish we didn't and is causing bad things to happen. The idea that "drinking is bad" is entirely evidence based but it is totally at odds with "drinking is good" which has been incredibly deeply learned over a long period of time because it is fixed in place by elevated dopamine levels that accompanied the drinking sessions. But "drinking is good" is flawed memory; it is an amplification and fixation of the brief respites that alcohol gives us from the distress that is itself caused by alcohol. Drinking might once have been a genuinely enjoyable experience but those days are long gone. Once we start to become alcohol-tolerant then our mood lowers and we need to drink increasingly more before we experience any lift in our spirits. Eventually our mood becomes so depressed by alcohol-tolerance that we can't drink enough to become happy. But even though drinking no longer brings real happiness that elevated dopamine level still reinforces the memory "drinking is good" because life is better than it was before we drank. The memory is shared across a plethora of places, times and occasions but the consistent theme linking them all is that drinking is a good thing and this becomes something we come to know more firmly than anything else. The power of this feeling and the absence of supporting detail are simple to demonstrate. If we went to a Doctor for some problem and they prescribed a medicine that meant we had to stop drinking for three months then we would be completely horror-struck. There is no supporting reason or rationale for this reaction, there is only instant and overwhelming fear. All logic and information support taking the medication but this doesn't prevent the instant reaction of horror: the strength of the emotion associated with stopping drinking overwhelms the logic. The difficulty our mind has in resolving the conflict between "drinking is good" and "drinking is bad" is that only one side is negotiable. As we drink more the evidence that "drinking is bad" mounts and becomes irrefutable but the inner knowledge that "drinking is good" is still being reinforced. As our circumstances worsen the two positions become even further polarised and the stress caused by this dissonance becomes increasingly severe. But this internal turmoil is only one source of alcohol-related distress, there are others; secrets, lies, guilt and shame.

The stress we suffer with secrets is that for every secret there is the worry that it will be discovered; fear we will be seen somewhere we're not supposed to be, fear our hidden drink supply will be found, fear we will be discovered drinking secretly and so on. But we don't just accumulate secrets from trying to hide our drinking we also make them from the consequences of drinking. While we are drunk our judgement is so impaired that we do things we would never normally do, we do things we are deeply ashamed of, and we add these guilty secrets to the ones we already have. Holding secrets is its own mental burden but concealing these secrets also involves lies, and these too have to be guarded. As our secrets and lies grow in number and magnitude so does the effort involved in keeping them, and this burden builds into a persistent sense of fear; fear that our secrets and lies will be discovered and fear that we will be exposed as not the person we present ourselves to be.

Secrets cause us to accumulate anxiety and fear but the extent to which we are troubled by our existing concerns also grows. The flight-or-fight response heightens our alertness and focusses attention to identify the danger for which our body has been prepared. But our senses find no apparent danger so our brain trawls through unresolved issues and brings them forward to see if these are the source of the alarm. Our mind cycles through all the unsatisfactory issues in our life, past and present, and attempts to bring then to a better conclusion. As we dwell on our problems our mind reaches out to find to other information that might help to resolve them and this makes our problems beget more problems; but most of them remain unresolved. Many of these concerns happened in the past so can never be changed but we still replay the scenes over and over in our mind desperately trying to find a better conclusion. These worries not only persist, we also strengthen them. Constantly re-visiting and replaying scenes from the past makes the neural pathways containing these memories firmer and faster to access and they come back into mind far more easily. Anxiety caused by our alcohol-tolerance causes issues with unsatisfactory outcomes to churn endlessly and every time we dwell on one we re-build all the emotions associated with it; guilt, shame, fear, anger, and resentment.

While the stress from secrets, lies, and worry are consequences of our own actions there are also stresses from external influences; they are in response to how we think other people see us. Normal drinkers have a completely different daily experience to us when it comes to alcohol. They do not have an out-of-control reward system, their memories are not hopelessly biased in favour of alcohol, their mood hasn't changed in response to regular drinking, and their ability to freely choose to drink or not drink is intact. This has a direct bearing on how people judge us. Things like praise, guilt, sin, and shame are only applied to actions that are freely willed. I.e. only actions that are freely chosen are seen as deserving of credit or blame. Normal drinkers expect that we have the same free-will regarding alcohol that they do, so they believe we have *chosen* this course of action and therefore deserve condemnation. The consequence of this accusation for the recipient is shame: being accused of drinking too much heaps shame on us. We recoil from it aggressively and we begin to change our behaviour to avoid this disgrace.

We evolved to live in communities and a part of that evolution is that we adopt the standards and behaviours of the community. We aid our survival by being in a group, so we serve the aspirations of the group as well as our own; this is how we win the support of the group. The way we evolved to make our behaviour to conform to that of the group is that our minds punish us when we fail to meet the group's standards. We feel regret, guilt and shame when our behaviour is not aligned to that of the group and our drinking definitely does not meet that standard. Bizarrely one part of our brain compels us to drink and then another part punishes us for doing so. The emotional discomfort evolved to encourage us to change our behaviour to conform to that of the group, but when it comes to our drinking we cannot. We can't because we can't do what is expected of us: we can't control our drinking. We can't stop drinking but the shame it brings is so painful that we find ways to get around the problem. If no single person ever sees the full extent of our drinking then our drinking can appear to fall within acceptable norms, so we adjust our behaviour to create this illusion. We drink somewhere and then move onto somewhere else for more, we drink in different places on different days, we buy alcohol in different places on different days, we lie about where we go, when, and for how long, we dispose of our empties discretely, and we hide alcohol and drink it unseen. This last point is further encouraged by one of the changes that came with becoming alcohol-tolerant: diminished social confidence. We hide alcohol and drink secretly because when we drink like this then nobody sees us; therefore we aren't shamed for it. But this can have a terrible cost. If we avoid social contact completely then the circumstances for being shamed don't arise and in this respect hiding away is successful. But this leads us to becoming increasingly socially isolated and ultimately we feel safer alone than we do in company: the prospect of meeting other people becomes confronting. This social withdrawal is not caused by alcohol, it is driven by shame.

We pursue a broad range of actions to hide the extent of our drinking in an effort to avoid shame but doing this increases the number of secrets we hold and it also increases the cognitive dissonance we suffer. All these manoeuvres divert other people's attention from how much we are drinking, but this also means that we actually recognise within ourselves that our drinking is problematic. Our actions are attempts to avoid attracting the shame of being labelled an alcoholic, but the very act of pursuing them adds weight to our own body of evidence that we probably are, and this increases the dissonance even further.

As our drinking becomes increasingly compulsive we reach the point where the distress of not having alcohol in our bloodstream is itself a driver of our behaviour: being sober brings on cravings. As we spend an increasing proportion of our time drinking we spend less time on activities we that used to enjoy. We stop doing things that don't involve drinking and we avoid doing things that require us to not drink for any significant part of the day. As there becomes less and less of our day that we don't drink, and as we do less and less of anything that makes us feel good apart from drinking, then alcohol becomes the only perceived goodness in our lives: not only do we believe that "drinking is good", over time it becomes the *only* thing that is good. More and more of our time becomes committed to drinking and to being functionally impaired as a result of that and our place in the world begins to slide backwards. We start failing to meet the standards society expects of us, and we start failing to meet the standards we expect of ourselves. By our own judgement and that of others we are failing as individuals; at work, at leisure, and at home. We accumulate regrets, and we do (or don't do) things that have increasingly significant consequences. Where once our drinking might have resulted in us feeling foolish and embarrassed there are now more serious consequences; lost jobs, lost opportunities, and lost relationships. There may also be problems with the law.

As our standing in the world declines the damage to our self-image is huge. How valued we think we are, how capable we think we are, how worthy we think we are, and how loveable we think we are all in decline. While we show the world a façade of confidence we are full of doubt internally and everything in our lives seems to be falling apart. Our problems churn endlessly in our mind but never get solved and we become haunted by a fear of failure. We don't understand how things have become like this and we can't shake off the incessant feelings of fear and anxiety. Nobody seems to understand how difficult things are for us and we feel desperately alone. If our minds go to the past we see the occasions we've been unfairly treated and if we look to the future we see only inescapable darkness and despair. We begin to feel that our problems are insurmountable and being constantly on edge looking for danger brings on a sense of impending doom. There seems to be no escape. Ultimately we feel like complete failures, utterly worthless, and life itself seems pointless. In response to all these stresses our minds scream at us to drink; it is the only thing that brings some relief.

Our addiction began with the reward system in a runaway state, was compounded by the changes in our brain that came with alcohol-tolerance and is then worsened by our psychological response to these. The inner stress caused by the conflict between "drinking is good" and "drinking is bad" becomes enormous and the shame, guilt and stress caused by holding secrets steadily accumulate. The stress caused by our day-to-day concerns is heightened and our fear of the judgement of others pushes us into isolation. We know we shouldn't drink so much; it would be good if we drank less, but all our other issues appear so demanding. We try to limit what we drink but our efforts seem to be completely ineffective and we struggle to understand this, but we have so many other concerns too and this is not our biggest. All of this builds into a torrent of distress that we experience when we are sober and when we feel these emotions we are triggered to drink to relieve them... and that drink makes us feel better. This gives us a bizarre perception of alcohol: we don't see alcohol as the cause of our problems; we see it as a solution to them.

There have been numerous occasions when we intended to not drink, or only have a couple, but the roaring demand to drink overwhelmed us... the cravings induced by our triggers are too powerful to resist when our whole mind screams "a drink will make you feel better!" This insistence is even more compelling because it is true; we *will* feel better if we have a drink; we will become happier, we will feel less socially isolated, we will feel more care-free, and we will feel calmness replacing the tension and stress. But as soon as we are sober again we are once more consumed by fear, anxiety, confusion, frustration, and loneliness and drinking is the only relief from them that we know. Our reward system builds triggers for all our anxieties and we are compelled to drink to relieve our discomfort. Once we begin drinking then we are compelled to continue. This means that we increasingly invest our time and money in drinking. We drink when we should be doing things with and for other people, and we spend money on alcohol that should be spent elsewhere. It appears to the onlooker that that we are indulging ourselves before considering others, but this is not how it seems to us. They see us wasting time and money on drink, but for us, without exception, every single time we that drank we were earnestly motivated to do so and the reasons our mind gave us to do so seemed perfectly convincing. To us our drinking is not self-indulgent; there is always a perfectly reasonable justification for having a drink. Our altered reality becomes that drinking is always warranted and the burdens of our decline continue to mount.

As it becomes increasingly necessary to change the way we are drinking it also becomes increasingly difficult to do so. There is no sudden dividing line at which somebody either is or isn't alcoholic. Alcoholism is progressive and develops very slowly; it creeps on so slowly that we are unaware of the changes within ourselves. Also, because it is a progressive illness, not all alcoholics experience or exhibit the same severity of symptoms; some are sicker than others. But in general terms the longer we have been drinking heavily then the more entrenched our addiction becomes and the more our brains adapt to offset the regular presence of alcohol. But we aren't directly aware of any of this. We can only recognise a long term trend of a gradual increase in the amount we drink. We do not see the change in our mood, we do not notice the increased pre-occupation with thoughts of drinking, and we do not directly link our anxiety, stress and depression with alcohol. The way our brain works and the thoughts that dominate our mind have shifted, and these shifts cause changes in our behaviour. What we don't recognise is the extent to which this changed thinking and behaviour is *caused* by our drinking.

As our addiction develops we step through a series of observable behaviour changes:- morning shakes becomes regular, we start to drink before a drinking occasion, and we want to continue drinking when it's time to leave. We drink at inappropriate times, we lie about how much we drink, when and where, and we don't want to discuss our drinking. We miss work or family obligations, we hide alcohol, we agree to drinking limits but don't keep to them. We behave out of character when drinking, drinking becomes more important than eating, we surround ourselves with heavy drinkers, we drink early in the morning, and we attempt periods of abstinence.

While these are changes that might be noticed by others, we keep far more to ourselves. In the face of mounting distress, anxiety and depression we carry on pretending that nothing is wrong, but inside we have a growing sense that *everything* is wrong, and while there is a progression of indicators visible to those looking on there is another private escalation of changes that we are aware of but conceal from public display:- we find we've lost the ability to control how much we drink once we've started, we are irritable, nervous or uncomfortable when not drinking, and we routinely experience memory loss or blackouts. We sneak drinks and lie about how much we actually consume. We get anxious when people talk about those who drink too much, and we drink to relieve uncomfortable emotion and distress. We are uncomfortable in situations where there is no alcohol, we drink as a reward for even small achievements, our waking thoughts are of alcohol and we *need* the first drink of the day. We have unreasonable feelings of resentment towards other people and the world, we think of getting away as way to stop drinking, we regularly drink alone and our guilt extends into constant remorse. We think about alcohol all the time, we lose our moral compass (we start doing things we wouldn't have considered previously), we become angry when our drinking is discussed and we have a reflex denial that our drinking is a problem. We experience fear that is not attached to any apparent threat, we can't imagine a life without alcohol, and we feel desperately alone, irritable, confused, depressed and scared. We suffer extremely low self-esteem, we have a sense of complete hopelessness and impending doom and we have suicidal thoughts.

As our addiction progresses so too does our mental un-wellness. Deep down we know that something is wrong with our drinking but we have other problems too. Every aspect of our lives is unravelling and in addition to that there is a mounting burden of shame and guilt. We drink secretly, hiding it from the sight of others;

this is the only way we can drink as much as we need to without being shamed. We do things that offend our own consciences time after time and the list of our regretted actions is beyond counting. We are completely confused as to how we've reached this point and the massive burden of secrets, lies, guilt and shame keeps increasing. We can't stop thinking about our troubles unless we have a drink. Our brains are so adapted to the presence of alcohol that there is a massive oversupply of glutamate and a deficit of GABA. This has become essential in order to keep our brain functioning adequately when we drink, but when we are not drinking our mind is a roaring and tumbling torrent of unresolved issues, bad outcomes and guilty secrets. We play and re-play scenes in our mind to try to find different resolutions, but they do not come, so the issues spin and twist and churn endlessly. We feel impossibly alone and scared; scared that our secrets will be found out and scared that this is it... this is all our life has amounted to.

Our social confidence becomes so low that we feel detached and apart from other people and this aloneness is crushing. Even though we are surrounded by people, at home and at work, no-one seems to see how hard our life has become. Alcohol is the only thing that gives us relief from our problems and it is the only thing that makes life bearable. No-one understands and no-one is coming to help; we are on our own. We can't control or limit our drinking; we've tried many, many times and failed completely. Stopping drinking is impossible; we've tried to stop for periods but usually only managed a few days so it seems like we are trapped with no possibility of escape. Our position is completely hopeless; that is, we are without hope. Permanently stopping drinking might improve our position but a life without alcohol is utterly unimaginable... it is the only thing that relieves our suffering; it is the only thing that makes life worthwhile.

For its addicts alcohol steals the joy, meaning and purpose from our lives in exchange for an empty promise of fun, and it appears to be completely inescapable.

Denial

The Oxford English Dictionary defines denial as "a refusal to accept that something unpleasant or painful is true". Denial in alcoholism is often used to suggest that the individual refuses to accept the harm that alcohol is doing; but this grossly misstates the issue. This suggests that we choose to be stubborn rather than to accept the facts, whereas the actual difficulty is that we give insufficient weight to the truth; we do not deny the facts... we find them unconvincing. Denial is not stubbornly refusing to accept what we don't want to hear, it is that our mind has contradictory ideas that it finds more convincing and these contradictory ideas and memories are created by mental functions that are distorted by regular and heavy drinking. Denial is a *symptom* of addiction.

People close to us try to convince us that our drinking is bad and that we should change it, but this has no apparent effect. Those observing or trying to help us are completely baffled by this... "why don't they see all the harm that their drinking is doing?" They think we are being weak, stubborn or selfish. They see all the problems that our drinking is causing; to ourselves, to our families, at work or with the law and the solution is obvious to them... drink less! But they form this conclusion based on their own response to alcohol, and the way we see it is entirely different. We don't disagree with the facts, we see the same problems as they do; we drink more than we should, we drink more often than we should, we spend time drinking when we should be doing other things, and bad things happen as a consequence of our drinking. For them that is the whole story, but we know some other things too. We know that "drinking is good!" and "drinking is fun" and we know these more firmly than anything else; this knowledge is false, but it seems real and is incredibly deeply learned. We also know from the balance of our memory that drinking represents fun and good times; the good memories of drinking are enhanced and the memories of bad experiences are suppressed. What is also becoming increasingly apparent to us is that we are unable to "drink less"; that ship has sailed. But we know with absolute certainty that a drink will make us feel better. We aren't necessarily aware that we feel anxious, alone, miserable and distressed *because* of our drinking, but we *do* know that a drink will make all of these go away. These things are all products of our addiction and normal drinkers don't have them. But they don't simply compete with the evidence that our drinking is harmful, they are also more persuasive. The "drinking is bad" side of the argument has words, events, places and people associated with it; it is information and evidence based. But the "drinking is good" side of the argument doesn't come as a neatly formed package of well-constructed argument. It doesn't have words it has feelings; desires, urges, yearnings and cravings, and we can't prevent them from coming. We can protest and challenge them as much as we like and we can construct the most persuasive of arguments but the feelings persist. The feelings are generated independently of conscious thought and they are impervious to reason; we can't debate or negotiate with them and facts do not diminish them. Not only are these feelings untouched by evidence, they arrive first: we *feel* that having a drink is a good idea before our higher mental functions even begin to compile evidence that drinking now or drinking more might be unwise. But the feelings go even deeper. The feelings don't just tell us that drinking is good they tell us that drinking is the *only* thing that is good and that there is no fun in life without alcohol.

We can't imagine life being worthwhile without alcohol. Under these conditions we do not reach the same conclusion about our drinking as normal drinkers do. It makes no sense to us to stop drinking when, as far as we are aware, drinking is not only a good thing it is the *only* thing that makes us feel better.

We uphold the position that "drinking is good" far, far longer than is rational and objective. In fact we are neither rational nor objective when it comes to alcohol because our distorted minds lead us to flawed conclusions. But as our daily experience of life worsens the weight of argument steadily grows on the "drinking is bad" side and the distance between the opposing viewpoints becomes huge. On the one hand there is "alcohol is the only thing that makes life worthwhile" while on the other is "alcohol is destroying my life". The dissonance caused by this conflict silently torments us and it is this discomfort that causes us to react angrily when someone is critical of our drinking; they are poking at what is already a sore point. When they do so we try to make our behaviour appear reasonable in whatever ways we can. Our drinking pattern draws comment and we have many responses ready to go at a moments' notice:- "Everybody drinks", "If you had my problems you'd drink too", "It's not illegal is it", "Problem? What problem", "I'm not that bad, all I want is a little relief", "I'm not hurting anybody but myself", "I can stop any time I want to", "I'm not nearly as bad as other people", "Nobody is going to tell me what to do" and "I can handle it myself". But while we try to minimise any criticism directed at us we can't completely dismiss the evidence out-of-hand; facts are facts. It is perfectly apparent that our drinking is bringing unwanted consequences and we try to do something about this. Stopping drinking completely is an unthinkable idea because in our own minds alcohol is the only source of fun we know; stopping drinking means taking away all enjoyment from life. So while we can't consider stopping drinking we *can* keep trying to drink less and we make many, many attempts to do precisely this. We try everything we know to change our drinking; we change what we drink, we change where we drink, we try to limit the amount we drink at any one time, we try to only drink at certain times or on certain days, we try to stop for a spell... but nothing works. We repeat this time after time trying one way then another to bring our drinking under control but the result is always the same; we end up drinking exactly like we did before. Controlling our drinking is not an option available to us because it cannot be done; the gross imbalance and power of the reward system, our altered mental state brought on by alcohol-tolerance, and our biased memory make this impossible. Even though we can come to the intellectual decision that we have to drink less this has no impact whatsoever on the reward system because the reward system operates before, and entirely independently of, conscious thought. The reward system is completely unaffected by our intellectual decision to try to reduce the amount and frequency of what we drink. It still wants us to drink, it still wants us to drink more, it still wants us to drink now and it uses dopamine to compel us to do so. When we try to reduce our drinking and defy cravings then the pressure of the cravings mounts and they keep coming. Our minds pitch "drinking is bad" (supported by evidence) against "drinking is good" (supported by feelings) and the persuasive strength of feelings makes "drinking is good" prevail. But this conclusion leaves an unsatisfactory gap. There are facts on the "drinking is bad" side but few equivalent facts to support the "drinking is good side", so our mind steps in to try and find facts that fill this void.

Our mind actively generates plausible rearrangements of facts to justify drinking and by doing so reduce the dissonance. Whenever we try to manage our drinking our mind actively works against us and sabotages any attempt to either reduce what we drink or stop for a spell. Our mind actively *encourages* us to drink and it supports denial. While we attempt to avoid shame by telling other people things that make our drinking appear more acceptable our mind creates plausible reasons that encourage us to drink again: it creates evidence for the "drinking is good" side of the argument. Drinking more at a time when drinking is causing us so much difficulty isn't easy to justify, so there are only a limited number of ways to spin this positively and most alcoholics experience exactly the same arguments within their own minds:-

"Just one won't hurt" This justification is a trap; just one *will* hurt. If we have one drink then we have placed ourselves in the presence of alcohol and this causes drinking triggers to fire relentlessly. Not only do the cravings come as soon as our glass is empty they come with incredible intensity as the power of the craving depends on how close we are to alcohol. So once we start drinking we are powerfully compelled to

have another and our intent to have "just one" is crushed.

"Perhaps you weren't that bad" Sustained sobriety is built on three pillars; that it is necessary to stop drinking, that it is possible, and that it is worthwhile. This justification strikes at the idea that stopping drinking is necessary. The abject misery of our existence while drinking is actively faded with the passage of time and with it so does our resolve. The necessity of our course becomes less certain, but actually, nothing has changed... it only appears to have done so. This justification appeals to the idea that we can enjoy drinking if we only control it properly this time. But this idea is truly preposterous. We cannot control our drinking. We have attempted this countless times and failed every time. Another attempt will not bring a different result.

"You've done well, you deserve a drink" This idea comes when we've decided to give drinking a rest for a period, whether it's a few hours or a few days. Withdrawal begins when we don't drink and this raises fear, restlessness, anxiety etc. This is when this idea pops up, but it is both an excuse and a lie. Having a drink is *not* a good way to reward ourselves for not having had a drink... this is a lie, and inventing a reason to celebrate is an excuse.

"Poor me!" Self-pity corrodes our determination to not drink: "Poor me, poor me... pour me another drink!" If we start feeling sorry for ourselves then we dwell on our problems and when we dwell on our problems then related issues are also brought to mind. Soon our life appears to be nothing but problems. When we feel sorry for ourselves we bring on distress and once we have become alcohol-tolerant then distress is one of the most commonly activated and powerful drinking triggers that we have. We bring on intense cravings when we feel sorry for ourselves and we do this entirely within our own minds; no external stimulus is involved.

"No-one will know" This justification is a complete misdirect. The "no-one will know" justification is not about alcohol, it is about shame. Our real problem is that alcohol is destroying our lives, whereas shame is about being seen to be drinking in ways that others don't approve of. The idea is that if we drink and don't get seen then we can avoid being shamed. This justification causes us to drink secretly, which allows us to drink more without accumulating shame in the short

term but it also deepens our addiction and adds more to our burden of lies, guilt and secrets. Drinking secretly does not avoid the angst; it moves it to later on and makes it worse.

The last justification is also one of the most insidious: **"A drink will make me feel better."** This one is the most challenging to deal with because it is completely true. Drinking *will* make us feel better in the short-term but it makes the problem even more severe in the longer term. This justification however explicitly targets one of our vulnerabilities: we strongly discount the value of something later over the value of something now. It is enormously convincing.

The reward system continues to operate precisely as it did before regardless of what drink-related conclusions we have reached. It operates entirely independently of any conscious thought processes and our brains launch unbelievably compelling cravings when we don't drink. If we resist the cravings then our mind generates plausible seeming reasons why we should drink, and why we should drink now. Once we start to drink then we are in the presence of alcohol (we are close to it) so the intensity of the cravings is magnified and we are vigorously encouraged to continue.

We cannot moderate or control our drinking. Once our brains have become alcohol-tolerant then we already lack the means to manage how much we drink. This is an absolute truth; no-one has ever managed to overcome this. It was written in 1939 that "Physicians who are familiar with alcoholism agree there is no such thing as making a normal drinker out of an alcoholic. Science may one day accomplish this, but it hasn't done so yet." This is still true. Despite countless failed attempts to moderate our drinking we still keep trying because the thought of being without alcohol is so appalling to us. But we can't control our drinking and we never will because we lack the means to do so. There is a simple and obvious proof that we have lost control of our drinking, but denial prevents us from recognising it: if we *could* control our drinking then we would have done so a long time ago.

For as long as our minds uphold the ideas that "drinking is good" and "drinking is fun" then we also collect any evidence that supports this. Our minds arrange denial around three fundamental ideas: stopping drinking is not necessary, stopping drinking is not worthwhile, and stopping drinking is not possible. While these ideas prevail then stopping drinking serves no purpose. But these three ideas all have something in common and that is that they are all false; they appear real, but they are false. The idea that stopping drinking is not necessary is supported by evidence that other people drink, some people drink more than we do and that we don't look like alcoholics: alcoholics live under bridges, are dirty and drink from brown paper bags. That stopping drinking is not worthwhile is supported by the feeling that there is no fun in life except in drinking. If we stop drinking then we believe we are destined to be miserable for the rest of our lives; we have a terrible fear-of-missing-out. And the idea that stopping is not possible is based on our own experience... it doesn't matter what we try, or how hard, we always end up drinking the same as before. Denial is woven from a fabric of lies, yet even though these ideas are false we believe them completely and dissonance continues to polarise until we end up trapped in a position where we can't stop drinking, but we can't carry on either.

All alcoholics face this time of extreme inner conflict when the primal insistence that we continue drinking is challenged by irrefutable evidence that our continued drinking is disastrous. We are presented with what seems an impossible choice, but normal drinkers can't see this position. They look at all the harm that our drinking is causing and to them the choice is both simple and obvious: stop drinking! But it is far from obvious to us. We do not think we should stop drinking because our memory tells us otherwise, our feelings tell us otherwise and the justifications echoing in our brain tell us otherwise. When someone suggests that we should stop drinking then what we hear is that they want us to give up happiness for the rest of our lives. What our brain says is that drinking is fun, drinking is the only fun we know, so to be completely without alcohol is unimaginable to us. To us a life without alcohol means a life without fun... forever, and that is a terrifying thought. Who would willingly choose this option? To be willing to give up fun forever requires that the alternative is even worse. So we continue to drink and the alternative does precisely that, it gets worse.

Eventually our denial begins to break down. The first of the three ideas to fail is that "Stopping drinking is not necessary". This idea is supported by the hope that if we just try a little harder then we will be able to control and limit how much we drink and how often. What we are really seeking is a way to carry on drinking but without all the trouble that comes with it. We persist with this belief for as long as is humanly possible, because if we acknowledge that we are unable to control our drinking then the remaining alternatives are utterly appalling; we either carry on drinking and things get worse and worse and worse, or we stop drinking and are condemned to be miserable for the rest of our lives. But eventually we become so desperate to escape the misery of our entrapment that we will try almost anything to break free of it and *that* is when denial collapses. When denial is broken, then and only then, does recovery become possible.

Who becomes an alcoholic?

The preceding chapters of this book describe alcoholism; how it starts, how it develops, and how some people are captured by it. But while most people that drink do not become alcoholics, some do, and for them this attracts great shame. Shame causes us to lie about our drinking, hide our drinking and drink secretly, but shame is also responsible for our deep need to understand *why* we drink like we do. The reason for this is that shame is only attributed to actions that are freely chosen. If those actions are *caused* rather than chosen then no shame is warranted, and this is why we are desperate to find an explanation for our otherwise irrational behaviour.

Research shows that much of the likelihood that addiction will form is inherited. The simplest and most compelling evidence for this comes from studies of children born to alcoholic parents but raised in non-alcoholic families. Children born to alcoholic parents but adopted into non-alcoholic families are far more likely to become alcoholics than the average across the whole population. This increased likelihood of addiction isn't just a little, it is huge; it is as much as ten times the average. Another study demonstrates that adoption itself is not the cause of this as the adopted children of non-alcoholic parents only suffer alcoholism at the normal rate. So it is not the distress of adoption that makes alcoholism more likely among children of alcoholics, nor is it being raised in a heavy-drinking environment (which is not present once they have been adopted), it is the inherited genes.

We inherit genes from our parents but we are not identical clones. Our parents' height for example does not exactly determine our own, nor does them having a particular talent mean we that will have it too. The same applies to vulnerability to addiction; having one or more alcoholic parents does not mean that we will be alcoholic too. Just because our parents have the particular mental characteristics that favour addiction does not mean that will have them, and actually those particular characteristics aren't even uncommon. The principal characteristics that favour addiction are; strongly preferring the benefit of something over its detrimental consequences, and strongly preferring a result now over a result later. But these are not unusual characteristics at all, in fact everybody has them to some extent, it is only how strongly they are expressed that varies. Both of these characteristics are strongly expressed in potential addicts. This occurs completely routinely in the general population and can occur regardless of whether or not we have alcoholic parents.

Having parents that are alcoholics does not mean that we are pre-destined to follow that course, we are not. Alcoholism itself is not directly inheritable, it is only the characteristics that favour susceptibility that *may* be. Equally, the coincidence of these same characteristics can occur perfectly randomly. But having alcoholic parents does make it more likely than average that their children will both have the characteristics that favour addiction and also that they will be raised in an environment where heavy drinking is the normal behaviour: the susceptibility is likely to exist *and* this susceptibility is very likely to be engaged. A family history of addiction is found in 50% - 60% of all alcoholics.

There is still a great deal to be discovered about the specific genetic components of addiction but among current research there is significant focus on a condition called alexithymia: a reduced ability to identify, define, and explain our own emotions. It has been shown to be a vulnerability factor for addiction, and also that it precedes addiction rather than being a consequence of it. Symptoms of alexithymia include; poor emotional regulation, interpersonal problems, reduced social networks, and anxiety and depressive disorders, all of which seem very familiar to alcoholics. It is often an inherited condition and is particularly prevalent among those with a family history of alcoholism. Alexithymia is present in 6% - 10% of the general population, but in as many as 78% of alcoholics, and this is far too large a variance to be coincidental.

It is beyond doubt that vulnerability to addiction is to a significant extent inheritable. It is also clear that the two characteristics favouring addiction are not rare, they are perfectly commonplace. What is less clear is the extent to which our individual personality traits encourage susceptibility to addiction. Individual traits have been comprehensively studied in efforts to identify the "addictive personality", but the results of this research are indicative rather than conclusive. Personality traits are somewhat elective rather than rigid in that we can choose whether or not to deviate from them. Nevertheless there are personality traits that are more commonly grouped among alcoholics than the general population. Some of these characteristics are clearly the results of addiction rather than causes; compulsive behaviour, a very poor self-image and guilt are all direct consequences of alcoholism. Other personality traits that are more pronounced among alcoholics than the remaining population include impulsiveness and lack of patience. These indicate people who seek to be happy now rather than holding out for better things later on and are consistent with the underlying characteristics of strongly favouring benefits over disadvantages and strongly preferring something now over later. But the significance of other personality traits more commonly found in alcoholics than in the general population is less clear. Alcoholics are more likely than normal to cope with stress poorly, have low frustration tolerance, and be excessively sensitive to criticism. They are also prone to feelings of isolation, a high level of anxiety in interpersonal relationships, and emotional immaturity. All of these are traits that favour addiction because they are all relieved by drinking and can therefore form self-reinforcing triggers, but the extent to which they are causal of addiction is uncertain.

Just as there are personal characteristics that encourage addiction there are others that dis-favour spontaneous recovery, and the inability to correct problematic drinking is just as significant a part of addiction as susceptibility. Among the personality traits that are more significantly grouped among alcoholics are; ambivalence towards authority, independence, and being highly self-reliant. While these characteristics don't contribute to addiction they *do* diminish our ability to spontaneously recover from it. They make us less likely to value the opinion of others (doctors, therapists, counsellors etc.) and more likely to rely on our own opinions and resources. This in turn makes us less likely to accept advice or seek help and more likely to persist trying to solve the problem alone, and the longer we do this then the more committed our addiction becomes.

There are many studies of the distribution of alcoholism in society and they vary widely in the proportion of the population identified as adversely affected by alcohol. This large variation depends entirely on the criteria by which alcohol impairment is measured, and for the sake of simplicity, and nothing more, it is presented as 5% in the following text.

There is no single factor that pre-determines that we *will* become alcoholic, in fact it is *never* the case that we are predestined in this way. There are however some parts of the population in which alcoholism is more prevalent than the norm: alcoholism does not have an entirely random distribution. The great misconception in generalised addiction statistics is the assumption that the clustering around a particular factor is *causal* of addiction and this is often not the case at all. Youth for example is an oft-cited indicator: a very significant proportion of alcoholics started drinking in their early teens. From this many deduce that drinking young can *cause* addiction, but this isn't a secure conclusion. A very large proportion of people will drink unwisely when they are younger and many will drink far too much and too often. But most change their behaviour as they mature and do *not* become alcoholic. There are many social drivers of excessive drinking among young people but significantly the two primary characteristics that drive addiction; recognising benefits more strongly than disadvantages and favouring now over later are *normal* characteristics of adolescents. These usually recede at maturity and as they fade then drinking becomes steadily more moderate and controlled. Studies of alcoholics show that many drank from a young age, and studies of people that didn't drink at a young age show lower alcoholism rates; but the two are not as directly linked as may appear at first sight. Anybody can become addicted to alcohol if they drink a lot, and there are many reasons that someone might drink a lot, but most of these people will spontaneously recover if their circumstances change; 5% however will not. If you survey all alcoholics then you will find that most of them drank heavily in their youth, but if you survey all people that drank heavily in their youth (but were not from alcoholic parents) then only about 5% will be alcoholic: correlation is not the same as causation. Most people that drink to excess in their youth will develop drink-avoiding triggers and as they mature and these triggers progressively strengthen causing their drinking to slow down. Most people, though they might have drunk heavily when they were younger, will spontaneously change to a normal drinking pattern as they mature. Drinking heavily in our youth does not *cause* alcoholism, but it is very likely that people that end up as alcoholics also drank as teenagers... because most do.

An increased statistical likelihood of alcoholism also occurs around people that spend a lot of their time in environments where heavy drinking is a regular part of normal social behaviour. People who are raised in surroundings where heavy drinking is routine and people whose social lives revolve around heavy drinking conform to the normal behaviour of those groups, so they drink heavily too. Just as most people that drink in their teens do not become alcoholic most people that drink heavily because that is the normal behaviour in their social groups will change their drinking patterns if their social group changes. But again, 5% will not.

A third significant group of people in which alcoholism is more prevalent is people that are for some reason persistently and severely distressed. Alcohol-tolerance in most alcoholics causes changes in neurotransmitter release that lower our mood, make us less socially engaged and increase our anxiety. In us these emotional changes are caused by our brain adapting to drinking over a significant period, but some people are already in this state for other reasons. Childhood abuse or severe trauma can cause this as can unrelenting hardship or certain mental health issues. People who are persistently distressed like this may drink as a means to relieve their symptoms; aloneness, anxiety, and fear, shame etc and their drinking to relieve these emotions quickly forms powerful triggers. They build strong drinking triggers that fire whenever they are distressed (which for them is always) and this drinking to relieve their distress forms into the same self-reinforcing feedback loop that occurs with alcohol-tolerance.

This behaviour has been replicated in rats. Addiction begins and develops in the reward system and all animals that have a brain comprising two hemispheres have this reward system, so rats and mice have been the subjects of very many addiction experiments. Rats can become addicted by forcing them to drink heavily. If they are given no choice but to drink heavily (by only providing them water heavily laced with alcohol) then after a while their reward system directs them to seek and secure alcohol. If at this point they are given a choice of alcohol-laced water or plain water then the rats continue to drink the alcohol: they are addicted. But in this environment the rats are normally under significant duress; they are caged and entirely deprived of their normal environment. If they are placed in a comfortable and natural environment then they *do not* continue to drink the alcohol, they revert to plain water; that is *most* of them do. A similar result was seen in the soldiers returning from Vietnam. While enduring the distresses of war a huge number of these soldiers became heroin addicts, but on returning home most of them spontaneously recovered, *but some did not*. The ones that remain addicted, like the rats that didn't revert to water, are the ones that lack the means to recover spontaneously... the 5%.

The prevalence of alcoholism is higher in the three groups identified here than in the whole of society; those drinking heavily while young, those in social groups where heavy drinking is normal, and those who are persistently distressed. But these people do not necessarily all become alcoholics; very many will change their drinking behaviour perfectly spontaneously. Many young people will change their drinking behaviour as they mature, most people in heavy drinking social groups will drink normally if their social circle changes and many of those living in persistent distress will change their drinking patterns if the source of their distress is removed. In all these circumstances the majority of people are able to spontaneously change their drinking behaviour; but 5% do not.

The progression into alcoholism requires both drinking heavily over a sustained period *and* the absence of the means to stop. People that do not drink regularly will never undergo the changes in their brain that come with alcohol-tolerance so they will never become alcoholic. But some, and only some of those that drink heavily will, and this is very significant. The incidence of alcoholism is higher in the three parts of the population described above (youth drinkers, those in heavy drinking environments and the persistently distressed) than in the whole population, but they all have the same things in common: drinking heavily and drinking regularly. It is *this* that causes the prevalence of addiction in these groups. Drinking persistently doesn't *cause* alcoholism, what it does is it engages that vulnerability where it exists, and the progression to alcoholism continues from there. The same vulnerability may exist elsewhere in the population but if these people don't engage in regular and heavy drinking then that vulnerability is never exposed.

The things that create vulnerability to alcoholism are all internal; i.e. they are all contained within ourselves.

But there are some widely held beliefs that some external factors influence addiction. Specifically, advertising and widespread availability are often cited as contributing to alcoholism, but neither of these is the case. Alcoholics do not need advertising to encourage them to drink; we already create the need to drink within our own minds. Once we have become alcohol-tolerant then the demand that we drink comes from the consequences of being sober and no other stimulus is needed. Alcohol advertising does not *cause* addiction. This point is more obvious in the case of other addictive drugs. People become addicted to drugs like cocaine, heroin, and methamphetamine yet these are not advertised at all and you can't just nip to a local store to get them. Advertising may have an influence on the behaviour of normal drinkers but alcoholics are already going to drink anyway. Also the wide and easy access to alcohol does not cause addiction. Wide availability may encourage drunkenness, but not addiction. Alcoholics will go to extreme lengths to secure alcohol when they need it and whether or not it is convenient to access has no bearing on this. Making alcohol less available may have an impact on drunkenness but it has no impact on addiction. We do not drink because it is convenient; we drink because we are compelled to. Neither advertising nor wide availability are direct causes of alcoholism, but they do have a peripheral effect. Of themselves they don't cause addiction but they may encourage the heavy and persistent drinking that engages the vulnerability where it exists.

We had no way of knowing when we first drank that we were susceptible to addiction; we only did the same as everyone around us. We had no idea that we were initiating a process that would ultimately bring us to our knees, and there were no warning signs that this was happening until it was too late. Whether we inherited the mental characteristics that favour addiction or we got them through random variability makes no difference to the outcome. Once we drink regularly this leads to drinking more heavily and this is driven by the two crucial mental characteristics: greatly preferring the benefits of something over its drawbacks, and greatly preferring something now over something later. These two characteristics are neither created nor altered by drinking. We don't make them this way because we drink, we are born this way. We do not cause our alcoholism by drinking. Our only part in this is that we activated the susceptibility.

The longing to understand why we became alcoholic is driven by the need to avoid shame. If we drink because something compels us to rather than from making poor choices then we can avoid the shame of it. Understanding our addiction better can lift the shame we impose on ourselves but we cannot expect to remove the judgement of others. Most alcoholics only start to understand the nature of our condition as we struggle to confront it. We only seek out this knowledge when there is a need to know it and normal drinkers never have such a need. Their answer to the question "why don't they just drink less?" is complete and satisfactory from their untainted viewpoint and they don't need to research it further. We should not expect relief from judgement by people that do not know better because they have no need to know better. We fight off the designation "alcoholic" while we think that the cause of our problem is being a weak or bad person, but when we understand that our condition is not caused by poor control but by a condition causing the *absence* of control then we can accept it more easily. Shame obstructs seeking help and when we understand why we are the way we are with respect to alcohol then a huge burden of shame is lifted, a pillar that upholds denial is removed, and the barrier to seeking help is lowered.

Understanding the causes of our addiction may make it easier to bear but it doesn't change what has to be done. This knowledge does not undo the changes to neurotransmitter activity in our brain, it does not remove the triggers that have formed, it does not create the alcohol-avoiding triggers that did not form, and it does not rectify our distorted memory. The course of action required to become well again is the same regardless of how our addiction formed; first we have to stop drinking, and then we have to undo the damage caused. But until we get to the position that we can even contemplate stopping drinking then the wreckage continues. While we remain convinced that drinking is good and while our mind generates plausible reasons to continue drinking then we cannot stop; and everything continues to get worse and worse. But eventually as our decline continues there comes a time that our position is so desperate that we will try anything to escape the misery; denial collapses and eventually, somehow, from somewhere, we find the will to change.

Withdrawal

Our descent into addiction is so slow that its progress is largely invisible to us. The parts that we notice are; that we are definitely drinking more than we used to and that we are drinking more often than we used to. But there is a parallel decline that we notice but don't link to our drinking: as the amount we drink steadily creeps up then so do all the changes that come with alcohol-tolerance. We become less care-free and more beset by our concerns, our mood lowers, and our anxiety increases. Anxiety, fear, and depression are inevitable consequences of drinking heavily over a long period; they are opposite sides of the same coin. But we experience these independently of drinking so there is no way for us to directly associate this distress with our alcohol consumption, let alone recognise that the drinking may be the *cause* of the distress. It seems to us that we are often drinking because of all our worries, but that worry is to a great extent caused by our alcohol-tolerance. We worry when we are sober because of all the changes in our brain that come with alcohol-tolerance, this launches cravings, and then we drink. This has the appearance to us of drinking in response to our problems, but in fact we are drinking in response to being sober: we have "cause" and "effect" back-to-front.

As our addiction progresses then everything escalates: cravings get triggered by more circumstances and the cravings themselves become more compelling. The changes in our brain due to alcohol-tolerance become more severe, further lowering our mood and making us more irritable and even more socially withdrawn. We know we are drinking too much and we try to bring it under control; we try to drink less, we try to drink less often, we try to limit what we drink in a single session, we try moving, we try changing where we drink... but nothing works. We make commitments to others about drinking less and we make commitments to ourselves, but we can't keep them. We drink in ways that attract shame and the psychological defences we create to deflect that shame become more sophisticated. But nothing we do stops the drinking, so we try to hide it and our cravings and alcohol-tolerance form into a loop and strengthen each other. This progression is incredibly slow, it happens over years and decades, and it becomes seemingly inescapable: controlling our drinking is beyond us. We have tried absolutely everything we can think of and always failed, but life without alcohol is unimaginable: drinking is the only thing in our life that gives us a reprieve from hopelessness and we can't imagine our life without it. Our position seems inescapable and we are stuck in limbo; we can't carry on the way we are but we can't change it either. We keep on trying to bring our drinking under control, and we keep failing; it can't be done. We are aware of some truth about our position: we *have* lost control of our drinking and deep down we know this is true. But we can't admit this because that would make us one of those weak, worthless and useless people... alcoholics. We are perfectly capable in every other aspect of our lives, but not this one. For some inexplicable reason we can't fix this. We feel the weight of the implied shame of hiding our drinking; perhaps we *are* weak like people say, perhaps we *are* bad people, perhaps we really *are* useless... if we weren't we wouldn't drink like this, but we can't stop. It seems like we drink because we drink because we drink, there's no reason for it and there's no stopping it; it will always be like this and the future is impossibly dark. We've tried everything we can but there is no way out and this hopelessness pushes us into complete despair.

Something *has* to change or we will lose absolutely everything, but we are at our wits end. We have tried everything we know but are stuck in a state of confused hopelessness. We can no longer convince ourselves that our drinking is OK but we also know that we can't bring our drinking under control, so there is an obvious but terrifying conclusion. We start to think the unthinkable idea: we might have to stop drinking altogether, but the mere thought of this fills us with dread. There seems to be no supporting argument linked to this fear, there is only a deep and immediate dread, but the fear is very real. It is built on that deeply learned memory that "drinking is good", and the thought that we might stop drinking altogether gives us an instant and intense fear of missing out. Our mind responds "but that means no more fun... ever" but the alternative has become equally appalling. We can no longer dismiss or deny the damage that our drinking is doing and even the best of our justifications fails to be plausible. For most of us the day finally comes when denial falters and we start to entertain the possibility that we so don't want to accept... that we might be an alcoholic! When we start to acknowledge this idea then denial is weakening. While the fight is locked within our own heads it is irresolvable and eventually in desperation we tentatively reach out for other opinions. Most often it is what someone else says that tips the balance but it is not that they say something that is new and convincing, it is the timing of it, because only when denial is exhausted does anyone else's opinion carry any weight. It is not the words spoken that tip the scales on denial; it is when they are said. Eventually denial collapses and we decide: it has to stop! But this decision to stop drinking does not mean that we start to recover; it only means that recovery ceases to be impossible.

Stopping drinking is incredibly difficult but it is not the fight that we expect; our fight is not with the bottle but with our own minds and it is a fight we are ill-equipped to win. We are fighting ourselves and are therefore at best only the equal of the challenge, but the addicted part of our brain, the reward system, is armed with something that we have no effective counter for: feelings. We can't apply a superior argument that overcomes these feelings because feelings are impervious to reason. So while we may have made a conscious and considered decision to stop drinking this is the *only* thing that has changed. Our decision to stop has no impact whatsoever on the reward system which still compels us to drink at every triggering circumstance we meet, and we have hundreds of these. Our memory remains biased towards remembering drinking as a good thing rather than a bad one. Our mood is still depressed, we are still socially withdrawn, and our minds are a roaring, churning torrent of problems. The cravings are going to come, and there's nothing we can do to prevent that. Our memory will tell us we are missing out, and our mind insists that "a drink will make you feel better". This is the starting point of our effort to stop drinking. We can only try to overcome the cravings and sabotaging thoughts with willpower and logic, and our experience of trying to do this is very discouraging. In addition to the hugely compelling cravings our mind also moves to sabotage any attempt to stop drinking and the most challenging ideas are; "it isn't worth it if I am going to be miserable for the rest of our lives", "stopping drinking is impossible... I've already tried and tried but can't" and "maybe I wasn't that bad, I just need to try harder". These are the three themes behind the ideas that our minds present to make us drink again; it's not worth it, it's not possible, and it's not necessary. These have always caught us out in the past and if we are to have any success then we have to change how we address the problem: nothing changes if nothing changes. The most powerful thing we can do to make this attempt different to all the others is to abandon the idea that we can beat this alone. Every time we have tried to do this alone we have failed. If we want to improve our chances of success then we have to do something differently, and by far the single greatest thing we can do to help ourselves is to engage help, any help... all help we can find. The research shows that the likelihood of achieving a lasting recovery entirely alone is virtually nil.

The descent into addiction is slow and seamless, but the path out isn't; the experience of stopping drinking is a far cry from creeping and imperceptible change. Withdrawal from addiction is an aggressive, raw and volatile experience and the shock to our system when we first stop drinking is enormous. There are incredible cravings to overcome and our brain presents lies to encourage us to drink again, but in the first one or two weeks there are also some externally observable symptoms.

On the first day of stopping drinking we experience symptoms that are not at all unfamiliar; we've gone without drink for a day many times in previous efforts to stop so we know exactly what happens. These first symptoms are; shaking, jumpiness, anxiety and sometimes also nausea and abdominal pain. These are all direct consequences of the sudden absence of alcohol. While we drank regularly over an extended period our brain adapted to the slowing effect of regular and large doses of alcohol by increasing release of the chemicals of our flight-or-fight response: cortisol, adrenaline and noradrenaline. But when we suddenly stop drinking completely then our brain still continues to apply these counter-measures until it recognises that they are not needed. When there is no longer any alcohol slowing the brain down then the effects of these are fully exposed. Cortisol makes us wide awake, noradrenaline makes us alert for signs of danger and adrenaline makes the body ready for immediate response: our heart rate accelerates and blood is moved to the large muscles. In the absence of alcohol the noradrenaline over-excites our nervous system, and we tremble. Adrenaline diverts blood from the skin to our large muscles and increases our heart rate. This makes us pale in appearance but overheating internally, so we get cold sweats. The raised cortisol level irritates the stomach causing the cramps and nausea. These first symptoms of withdrawal are the result of the over-excited flight-or-fight response and drinking would normally make all these symptoms disappear, but when we don't drink we feel their effects directly. The same is the case for the other changes due to alcohol-tolerance. We now no longer spend part of the day lifted from feeling down, alone and anxious. We also don't slow our brain down with alcohol so the accelerating effects of more glutamate (the accelerator pedal) and less GABA (the brake pedal) hit us fully, and the result is a hyper-active brain. Our brain runs fast and constantly churns over and over our problems; the chatter in our heads is incessant. A side effect of this accelerated brain is that time seems to pass very slowly, and getting through the first few days of not drinking seems to take forever. Not only are the days long, the nights are long too. We were already suffering from significant long-term fatigue caused by elevated cortisol preventing us from achieving deep sleep, but without alcohol slowing our brain down we find it is impossible to sleep at all. We lie awake, restless, hot and sweaty, with our minds racing around and around all our problems. Proper sleep *does* return, but not for a while.

The first cravings we get during withdrawal are from the triggers related to being sober and those related to our daily routine, so they fire automatically and continuously. During the day our mind races, we are fidgety, we can't calm ourselves, and the cravings come one after another. The cravings we experience are not only nearly continuous they are also the most powerful we have ever felt, and they are the most powerful because in the past we have always given in to them. We have rarely felt cravings at their peak before and now they *all* reach their maximum intensity and then we make them linger by thinking about drinking and this keeps re-firing those triggers. The reward system demands that we drink, our minds actively encourage doing exactly that, and the familiar taunts keep coming to us; "just one won't hurt", "you've done well, you deserve a drink", "a drink will make you feel better", and "no-one will know!"

Over the years of drinking our bodies adjusted to be in a perpetual state of readiness for action, this was to offset the impairment of the alcohol that would come. When we drank then the brain slowed the flight-or-flight response which in turn slowed the release of cortisol, noradrenaline and adrenaline and we relaxed. But when we stop drinking we also stop this slowing down, so the reduced production of cortisol, noradrenaline and adrenaline no longer occurs and the release of these stays raised the whole time. This means that for the first few days of not drinking the levels of these three are not just elevated, they continue to rise. As withdrawal progresses the levels of cortisol and adrenaline continue to climb bringing on; higher blood pressure, further increased body temperature, unusual heart rate (palpitations), and sometimes even confusion. The severity of these symptoms is determined by the extent to which our brain adapted to our alcohol intake and these symptoms can make withdrawal hazardous for some people. Supervised medical withdrawal is usually encouraged for those with backgrounds of prolonged and very heavy drinking and those with other medical risk factors.

The peak of withdrawal is usually experienced at around Day 4 or Day 5 and the period with observable effects lasts roughly a week although this can be two or even three weeks depending on the individual; but it does not last forever... there *is* an end to it. The changes to our brain and body were in response to regular and heavy drinking and these changes start to reverse themselves out when alcohol is consistently absent. The first things to come right are the changes related to the flight-or-fight response. Over the course of one to three weeks the levels of cortisol, noradrenaline and adrenaline steadily move back to our pre-drinking levels and this brings some very welcome benefits. The cold sweats stop, our hearts stops pounding and most notably our sleep returns, but not only does it return it is different. Elevated cortisol levels have for years prevented us from achieving a proper deep-sleep state, and when sleep does come back it is deep, restoring and refreshing. But while sleep is the thing we notice the most it is something else that people around us see; our skin colour returns. As the levels of noradrenaline fall then the trembling stops. Then as the adrenaline levels drop our heart slows down and blood is released back to the skin from our large muscles; we lose the pale appearance and begin to look healthier again. But while our flight-or-flight response steps down quite quickly it takes longer for our proper GABA and glutamate levels to restore themselves and even longer for serotonin and dopamine to return to normal. We are physically in much better shape than we were but we still have a racing mind and our mood is still low. We still have huge cravings that come nearly non-stop, and our mind is still churning and churning over our problems. All these symptoms would disappear if we only had a drink, and we know this! While we are fighting against the cravings our mind is actively working against us and the challenges return again and again; "Just one won't hurt", "you've done well, you deserve a drink", "no-one will know", "a drink will make you feel better". Of all the justifications our minds present it is that last one that is the most challenging, and it is the most challenging because it is completely true; a drink *will* make us feel better. Our minds also make us doubt ourselves; "you know you won't keep this up, you may as well have that drink now", "it's not worth being like this forever", "a drink will make you feel better"... "a drink will make you feel better"... "a drink will make you feel better". It is unrelenting.

We have previously only endured cravings for limited periods, but now they run the whole time and they all climb to their full strength. It is difficult to describe what the non-stop insistence of these cravings is like, but a crying baby is a fair comparison:- Imagine you are in a room. There is no-one else there except a baby, and the baby is crying. The crying is horribly piercing and incredibly irritating. You know you only have to pick the baby up to stop it crying but you are not allowed to. The screaming is excruciating, like the screech of nails on a chalk-board and it continues without pause. The longer you leave the baby alone the more insistent the crying becomes but even though it would be incredibly easy to pick it up and make the screaming stop, you must not. There's nowhere to hide and no way to get away from the screaming; it just goes on and on and on. You close your eyes, cover your ears, scream and shout to make it go away but it just keeps going. There's no escape from it, and no way to not hear it. Time passes incredibly slowly as the wailing and screaming just won't stop. The only way to make it stop is the thing you mustn't do, you must not pick up the baby, but who would know? Would it really hurt to pick it up to make the screaming stop for one minute? You could just pick it up for a short spell, nobody would know, you'd feel better for a few minutes. But you must not. It goes on all day, continues all through the night, carries on the next day, and the day after, and the day after that; there seems no end to it. It is agonising and never stops for more than a few minutes; then it starts again. It seems unbearable and almost impossible to resist the very simple thing that will make it stop... to pick up the baby... it would be really easy... that's all you have to do... nobody would know... nobody would know... nobody would know.

This is what cravings are like when we first stop drinking and this is how they should be. When we experience this then it confirms the unnaturally extreme extent to which our reward system has bound itself to alcohol and only when we stop drinking is this fully revealed. What we are experiencing in withdrawal is the extent to which our brain and body have adapted to offset the regular impairment of alcohol. But just as our brain changed to counter the effect of large and regular amounts of alcohol it changes again when that alcohol is no longer routinely present, and these changes happen faster than the decades it took to become alcohol-tolerant.

The initial withdrawal is marked by some physical discomforts but there has been an ongoing and larger internal struggle against cravings which continues throughout. As we resist the cravings then our mind steps in to try to convince us to drink and this is by far the greatest challenge in stopping drinking. The test is not so much the physical aspects of cravings and withdrawal but what happens inside our own heads.

The internal fight through withdrawal is relentless and at the same time as we are enduring the most severe cravings we have ever encountered our minds are trying to convince us that drinking is a good idea. We feel depressed, isolated, irritable, obsessed with all our problems, and sleep deprived. It is a perfect storm. It is no wonder that so many relapse in the first week of withdrawal, in fact it is remarkable that any manage to get through it at all; yet so many do, and eventually most will.

After withdrawal

The extreme measures our brain and body took to offset the impact of regular drinking are fully exposed when we first stop drinking and the result is shocking. We shake uncontrollably and may experience; stomach cramps, nausea, cold-sweats, headaches, a pounding heart, fear, anxiety, and a sense of aloneness. These are all changes that our body and mind made in order to try to keep us functioning effectively while we drank heavily. But these changes are not permanent and once we stop drinking these adaptations start to reverse themselves out. The flight-or-fight response steps down during withdrawal, first by reducing noradrenaline release and then by reducing adrenaline and cortisol. By the end of two or three weeks our flight-or-fight response has mostly returned to normal. Our liver and kidneys have had continuous days without struggling against an overload of alcohol, the body's accumulated toxins have been largely cleaned away, we are properly hydrated once again, and the physical change in our appearance is noticeable; our skin colour returns, our eyes are clearing, puffiness around the eyes is receding, we feel better and we stand taller. But this last change has nothing to do with hormones or neurotransmitters, it is caused by a change in our state of mind... hope has returned!

The changes that happened to our mind and body over years of drinking are layered on top of each other; an over-strengthened and polarised reward system, a biased memory, lowered mood, accelerated heart rate and elevated blood pressure, raised fear and anxiety, accelerated brain speed, a huge burden of guilt and shame, and psychological defences that counter any thoughts about stopping drinking. The flight-or-fight response is the first to change because its adaptations positively impair our performance once we stop drinking and these adaptations start to fade after about four or five days. The levels of noradrenaline, adrenaline and cortisol continue to normalise and a distinct marker is reached that shows that these have returned to their near normal positions; that marker is that sleep returns. As our days without alcohol accumulate then our cortisol level falls until it is no longer so high that it prevents sleep. Depending on the individual this happens somewhere between one and three weeks, but it is unmistakeable. Once our cortisol level drops to near normal then we are once again able to achieve a deep-sleep state that we haven't experienced in years. Not only do we suddenly get a full night's sleep, the sleep itself is different: it is refreshing and restoring. But while the flight-or-fight response steps down the cravings do not, they climb to a peak and it seems like they stay there. They *are* subsiding but they change so slowly that at first we don't notice the difference from one day to the next. It happens over weeks and months rather than days, but it *does* happen and this becomes clear with hindsight.

Cravings don't occur randomly; they are triggered. Certain circumstances, places, people, occasions and emotions are remembered by the reward system in relation to gaining alcohol. The brain recognises when these circumstances are present and launches the urge to approach alcohol and drink. These processes operate entirely automatically, we can't choose for this to happen or not, and once these triggers are established they are *never* forgotten: what has become known cannot become unknown. For the rest of our lives our reward system will scan what comes in through our senses searching for circumstances that match those that have previously yielded alcohol. When those circumstances are found our attention is drawn to the near-availability of alcohol and a craving is launched. We will forever have our attention drawn to alcohol when the circumstances match those of a trigger, but this does not mean that when we stop drinking we have to resist enormous cravings for the rest of our lives; we do not. Once the brain's reward system has identified a circumstance that yields alcohol then that trigger can never be removed, but what *can* change is the intensity of the craving that the trigger invokes.

The reward system aids survival but in the wild the availability of something beneficial like an important food can be unpredictable and the reward system accommodates this variability. For example, if we'd learned to sit under a tree because good fruit fell from it then the reward system would urge us to return to the tree and look for more food and this urge would strengthen each time we found food there. But if the tree stopped producing fruit then we would visit there forever if the motivating urges did not change and this would be an inefficient use of our energy. So the reward system evolved to be adaptable as well as compelling. Firstly, the cravings that are invoked have a limited time-span. If there isn't any fruit available at the tree when we visit then the urge to continue to search there fades after several minutes and so we lose interest and move on. Secondly, if things stop happening the way that a trigger anticipates then the importance assigned to that trigger is lowered. In exactly the same way that a trigger strengthens through repeated success it is weakened by repeated failure. When a trigger consistently fails to return the object sought then the importance of acting on it (the intensity of the craving launched) is reduced. The brain can't unlearn that something has been identified as something to be sought out, but the importance of securing it *can* be changed, and it is by successively denying cravings that we reduce their intensity.

By successively denying a craving the reward system recognises that the likelihood of a particular trigger being successful is less than anticipated and the urgency given to seeking out its subject is reduced. This is an incredibly important piece of information for anyone attempting to stop drinking:

Every time we resist a craving then the intensity of the next craving induced by that trigger is diminished.

The urge to drink lessens as we continue to deny the cravings and *this* is how we manage to stop drinking in the longer term. If this did not happen then the cravings would remain at their peak intensity forever and we would eventually fail because of the enormous effort required to continue fighting them off. We do not manage to stop drinking because we get better at resisting the cravings; we are able to stop drinking because over time the cravings fall to an intensity that we can overcome without undue effort.

The first cravings to lose their vigour are the ones that fire regardless of where we are or what we are doing; these are the ones that fire in response to being sober. When we stop drinking then we immediately feel the effects of our alcohol-tolerance and the triggers related to this fire automatically. Fear, agitation, anxiety, restlessness and alone-ness are all triggers that activate in response to us being sober and these triggers fire relentlessly when we first stop drinking. These are the source of the first cravings we encounter regularly and these are the first to lose their ferocity, but cravings do not change quickly. They diminish in strength as we continue to deny them but it still takes weeks and months to achieve a significant reduction. However, they *do* diminish and one day we look back and see that the cravings that once took everything we had to resist have faded and all but disappeared. By successively denying cravings from many triggers over an extended period our cravings for alcohol diminish to a level that doesn't disturb our daily passage through life. We still get them but we can step past them without being unduly distracted from what we are doing. When we successively deny the cravings then we end up yearning for a drink no more than, for example, a donut that we might see in a baker's shop window, or a strawberry, or some chocolate; the intensity of the cravings is back to within a natural range. But for this to happen we have to successfully deny the cravings from every trigger we encounter day after day, and when we first stop drinking the cravings are so intense that this effort is exhausting.

When we stop drinking we are not only confronted by the most intense cravings we've ever encountered, they are also never-ending. No sooner has one craving subsided than another begins; we can't escape from them and indeed we must not. In order to make the power of a trigger diminish it has to fail, and to make it fail we must first experience the craving and then not drink in response to it. But avoiding triggers altogether does not help us as it leaves them still at their full power. So if we are to move around freely in a world filled with triggering circumstances then we need to bring the intensity of the cravings down to a point that they are manageable, and to do this they have to be experienced and denied. Initially the non-stop assault of powerful and continuous cravings is exhausting and our resolve weakens when we are tired, but while fighting off the cravings takes enormous effort the launching of them requires none; it happens completely automatically. Our addiction is propelled by automatically generated urges and these urges are not only compelling (that is their express purpose) they also never get tired. Our mind's ability to launch cravings is limitless, but our resolve is finite. While we must expose ourselves to triggering circumstances in order to de-power the triggers we also need to manage our exposure to them so that we do not completely deplete our resolve because the fight against cravings goes on for months. The intensity of the cravings rises to a peak during withdrawal but only descends very slowly from there and we need to manage our exposure to triggers if we are to maintain sufficient resolve to prevail. It takes a huge and determined effort to confront and break down the strength of the cravings but over time it *does* happen.

Cravings are the main focus of our early struggle, but while we are completely absorbed by the severity of this challenge there are other changes that happen without any direct effort on our part or even our awareness. The flight-or-fight response steps down quite quickly but the other changes due to alcohol-tolerance persist throughout the discomfort of withdrawal and also through the first weeks of resisting the cravings. The altered GABA and glutamate have our mind racing and the reduced serotonin and dopamine keep us feeling low, stressed and alone. But when we stop drinking these four neurotransmitters are once again not at their best levels for optimal brain performance. Their displacement from the ideal is disadvantageous but it doesn't place us in peril like those changes to the flight-or-fight response so the urgency of adjusting them is lesser, but they *do* change over time. All of the changes that occurred to offset the regular and large quantities of alcohol are suddenly unhelpful when we stop drinking and the brain recognises once more that its effectiveness and efficiency are sub-par. The levels of dopamine, serotonin, GABA, glutamate, cortisol, adrenaline and noradrenaline are once again sub-optimal and as our days of abstinence lengthen these all begin to revert to pre-drinking levels. But none of these chemicals, neurotransmitter or hormone, has a single function; each performs many roles and these are all inter-related. These seven chemicals do not simply keep us performing better while drinking heavily they also play a part in regulating our mood, appetite, alertness, vigour and anxiety, and each now has to find a new level. Serotonin for example creates a sense of wellbeing and happiness but is also involved in digestion and regulation of sleep. Noradrenaline has other roles in the formation and retrieval of memory as well as glucose release, and cortisol also helps manage blood sugar levels and controls our salt and water balance. All of the main chemicals involved in alcohol-tolerance are linked to the others, working co-operatively for some purposes and competitively for others, and when they all start changing their base levels at the same time then there are some chaotic outcomes. While this is happening we experience very significant emotional turbulence. The period following withdrawal is an emotional roller coaster and as our brain works to find new optimal levels for each of the key chemicals of addiction we are also constantly exposed to massive cravings. But just as these slowly subside so too do the consequences of alcohol-tolerance.

Without the daily sedatory effects of alcohol we are quite suddenly exposed to emotions in ways that we haven't felt in a long time and they appear dramatic and vivid. We also experience alternate periods of high-alertness, lethargy, feeling good, feeling low, and so on. These fluctuations are a completely normal response to the sudden and complete absence of alcohol; they are caused by our neurotransmitter and hormone levels adjusting to find a new equilibrium. But these fluctuations also show us that our mind and body are un-doing the adaptations that were made when we became alcohol-tolerant. We don't have to do anything to make these changes happen and they continue to correct themselves for as long as we don't drink again. We tend not to notice these longer term changes because the changes are slow moving but there are a few exceptions to this, times that we *do* notice that something is different. The return of good sleep is one of them but another that is very pronounced (and quite obvious once we are alerted to it) is often referred to as the "pink cloud".

Shortly after stopping drinking we may experience a dramatic change in our demeanour; we become calm, bright and happy. This is partly due to the realisation that stopping drinking is actually possible (we are actually achieving what we previously thought was impossible), partly to do with the emergence of hope (hope that the future really *can* be better), but for the most part it is to do with changes to the release rates of the four neurotransmitters regulating our mood and brain speed; serotonin, dopamine, glutamate and GABA.

While we drank regularly and heavily our brain recognised it was over-producing serotonin and it reduced the amount being released and also the number of receptors detecting its presence. This led to us feeling miserable, stressed and anxious when we were not drinking. Our brain also released more glutamate (the accelerator pedal) and less GABA (the brake pedal) and these two combine to leave our minds racing and agitated. The release rates of dopamine, serotonin, GABA and glutamate each adjusts itself independently of the others but in the absence of alcohol they all reset themselves at the same time. As each seeks a new optimal level it first over-corrects, then under-corrects, then over-corrects again and so on in decreasing increments before settling onto its best release rate. When all of these reverse their positions simultaneously then this releases more serotonin more GABA and less glutamate, and these changes keep going until they become disadvantageous... they go too far. The effect of this first overshoot is quite dramatic. Our mind was accelerated and agitated but with more serotonin more GABA and less glutamate it becomes calm, and our mood that was for so long depressed, stressed and anxious gives way to feeling relaxed, happy and care-free. Our mind stops racing and our mood becomes bright. This is the 'pink cloud': a feeling of cheerful and calm well-being where everything in the world seems good. The first overshoot in particular is perfectly noticeable and if we experience it it puts us into an elevated state for an extended period; often several weeks.

The intensity and duration of the pink cloud varies enormously from person to person. Some have more alcohol-tolerance to correct than others, in some the changes happen faster or slower than others, and in some the changes will happen largely in unison but in others they won't be quite so synchronous. There is no way to know when it will begin, how heightened it will be, or how long it will last as this varies enormously from individual to individual, but the change to how we feel is perfectly apparent to anyone that experiences it.

The pink cloud shows that our brain is re-adjusting and undoing the adaptations made to offset the consequences of alcohol impairment. Our brain is adapting to being alcohol-free once more and is recovering, but it is not a smooth transition. During the pink cloud the world is a happy place and our troubles seem small. We have got through the fiercest phase of withdrawal and cravings seem to have receded somewhat, but this last point is incredibly misleading. Many of our most powerful drinking triggers are bound to distress; being unhappy, feeling alone, agitated, anxious and so on. But while we are on the pink cloud we feel neither unhappy nor distressed so while the pink cloud persists we are not triggered to drink so often... but this doesn't last. Our brain again recognises that the release rates of these four neurotransmitters level still isn't ideal and it adjusts them back a little. But this next time everything goes rather dull.

After the pink cloud period there comes a more sombre period. Our serotonin level dips a little, our cheerfulness drifts off to become a mild dissatisfaction with life and the cravings seem to come back. This can be an extremely challenging time and many fail to negotiate this dip. While on the pink cloud it seems like we have beaten our addiction but this is an illusion, there is still a long way to go. While on the high of the pink cloud everything is good and easy but when it fades we really feel the daily chore that staying sober has become and the effort no longer seems to bring the rewards that it did before. During this low phase it is typical that we doubt that our effort is worthwhile. The cravings still come very regularly and our brain still constantly insists that drinking is good, but we aren't happy like we were before. The cravings lack the ferocity they first had but they are still there and the daily grind of fighting them off takes its toll. We also suffer a drop in enthusiasm for our decision. When we first decided to stop drinking we had an extraordinary boost of determination that came from the desperate need to escape our hopelessness. But once our brain begins to undo the mood changes caused by alcohol-tolerance then that despair disappears and so too does the extra determination that it brought. Our ability to recall the depths of our distress is further diminished by Fading Effect Bias which actively reduces our recall of emotionally bad experiences. As our despair fades into the past then so too does the urgency of our cause.

Our determination declines and this lowering of resolve combines with a shift in the psychological manoeuvres that our mind presents. As the distress caused by drinking fades our mind presents the idea that control has been restored and two new themes of self-sabotage emerge: "you've beaten it now, perhaps you can have just one" and "maybe you weren't that bad after all".

The mood dip after the pink cloud is a very significant test and many that persevered though withdrawal will fall at this hurdle. But just like the pink cloud passes so does this lull and after that the fight settles into a more stable and progressively less demanding challenge... most of the time.

The following months

When we stop drinking permanently then our brain starts to undo all the changes that it made as it adapted to regular and large doses of alcohol. The brain adapted to large and regular doses of alcohol by changing the release of and sensitivity to certain neurotransmitters and these sort themselves out again with the passage of time. We weren't directly aware that they went astray and we aren't directly aware of them reverting other than that we slowly start to feel less miserable and less anxious. The brain spontaneously restores itself to an efficient working state but this recovery is not completely smooth. Serotonin greatly influences our mood and is in a state of flux once we stop drinking. At the same time as the brain is finding a new optimum level for this it is also finding a new levels for GABA and glutamate and the chemicals of the flight-or-fight response; noradrenaline, adrenaline and cortisol. Not only does each of these have to find a new optimum level, these levels also need to be found in relation to each other and a whole new overall equilibrium established. There are many chaotic outcomes as each adjusts itself relative to the others and the term "Post-

Acute Withdrawal Syndrome" (PAWS) refers to the period after withdrawal during which we experience erratic phases of mood and motivation which come and go unexpectedly. During this period we experience wild emotional swings; feeling low, feeling high, feeling restless or lethargic, and each episode can last a few days. In the past we drowned any emotional highs or lows in a blur of alcohol but now we encounter them raw, extreme and vivid. There is no apparent trigger for these episodes; we simply wake up one day feeling out of sorts, or teary, or fearful, or irritable, or with low energy. But if we persevere for a few days this will lift just as quickly as it started. After a while we learn to recognise the onset of these spells and develop the confidence that we will get through them because each episode, although challenging and confusing, is time limited. These intense emotional swings diminish over time but can occur for up to two years as the brain chemistry finally settles in on a new equilibrium.

After several months without alcohol there is still a fairly constant pull towards drinking, but the overall ferocity is diminished and it becomes manageable. All the triggers associated with our regular daily routine have lost their raw intensity and the problem has changed from being constant and compelling to a noisy clamour with the occasional spike of a fierce craving. The great challenge in this period is when we encounter triggers that have not yet been de-powered. At first the challenge is incredible as the cravings run nearly continuously and they are enormously powerful. But each craving resisted is progress, and over an extended period, months rather than days or weeks, the most commonly fired triggers lose their intensity... but *only* those! Infrequently met triggers still have most of their vigour. These can remain unchanged for years and sometimes contribute to relapse even after a considerable sober period; while we have taken the ferocity out of the triggers that we encounter frequently we still have a huge number of triggers that retain their full power.

In our time drinking we changed where we lived, where we worked, how we spent our free-time and so on. All of the triggers relating to these abandoned routines still have their full strength because we no longer meet those triggering circumstances and have therefore never taken any vigour from them. These triggers still hold their full power and occasionally we stumble across an old triggering circumstance, a powerful one, and the sudden intense craving we get is shocking. It is startling because we get a sudden intense craving out of nowhere and we are quite unprepared for it. These can come many months or even years after our last drink and our only defence against these is to know that they *will* occur at some point; it is to be expected. The good news with these is that they are few and far between and our resolve is typically in good shape by the time we encounter them.

We drive down the intensity of the cravings by applying enormous resolve over an extended period and over time the changes due to alcohol-tolerance reverse themselves out. But while our brain will restore itself spontaneously our mind does not. Alcoholism is viewed by society as a badge of worthlessness and as alcoholics this cuts very deeply indeed. But the distress associated with alcoholism isn't only due to the shame of being labelled an alcoholic it also comes from the efforts we take to avoid attracting the label. When we do that then we also accumulate secrets and guilt but there are other stresses too; our minds are strewn with the litter of the chaos and destruction that we have wrought. There are so many appalling things that we did and there are things that we should have done but did not. There are opportunities lost and there are aspirations destroyed; all caused by our drinking. These things actually happened and they are direct consequences of our addiction. But they do not disappear when we stop drinking; they leave an enduring toll.

It is surprising to many looking at addiction for the first time that the main effort of recovery programs is not to achieve enduring abstinence but to change the way that our mind works. There is no point in stopping drinking if our lives are still miserable, so abstinence itself is not the end-goal nor is it the same as recovery: abstinence is sustained cessation whereas recovery is becoming mentally well again. Success in recovery is not measured in time elapsed since our last drink it is measured in terms of mental wellness, and in that respect there is a lot to fix up.

There is far more to alcoholism than just maladjusted brain chemistry. The greater part of recovery is not actually breaking the hold of addiction and stopping drinking, it is repairing the psychological damage accumulated during our addiction and then learning to live in ways that don't re-engage our susceptibility. There is a burden of guilt that must be lifted if we are to recover to lead contented lives and there are two approaches we can take. We can either let the memories fade with time or we can confront them directly and work to permanently remove the pain of carrying them. While we live with major pain in our past then we are forever vulnerable to one particular piece of self-sabotage: "a drink will make you feel better". This is so problematic for us because it is completely true. If we are to live the rest of our lives free of alcohol then we also need to be free from the nagging pain of our past, and for one group in particular this is absolutely essential. For most people the path into alcoholism was first an un-balanced reward system that encouraged drinking heavily and regularly. This led to alcohol-tolerance lowering our mood which caused us drank to relieve that distress and this in turn created powerful distress-related drinking triggers. It was this that locked us into the trap whereby we drank to relieve the persistent distress that was itself caused by drinking. But some people are already in a persistently distressed state. People that suffer persistent distress for reasons other than alcohol-tolerance are forever at risk of returning to drinking regularly because if they ever drink again then they are immediately locked back into that self-reinforcing feedback-loop into hopelessness. They are at risk of this because when they stop drinking then they are relieved of the depression due to alcohol-tolerance but that does not leave them free of distress; they are still troubled. People that have problems other than alcohol that are causing persistent distress need to gain relief from these to be able to securely sustain lasting recovery, and this usually requires professional help. However, those that only have to deal with the psychological consequences of their own actions have two distinct recovery paths that they can follow.

Alcoholics carry a huge burden of shame and guilt and if unrelieved this will always steer them back towards drinking. One option is to simply wait and let the passage time dull the pain, the other is to deliberately engage with these issues and attempt to bring them to resolution. Most people engaged in a recovery program, whether it is institutional or community based, will attempt this resolution in one way or another. The process is extremely challenging. We have to look at our past, our secrets, and the things we did, and then bring them to a point that recalling them no longer hurts. This requires brutal self-honesty that is not easily summoned and it also takes courage and determined effort to achieve, but it is an important and often overlooked step in recovery. Being relieved of the distress of our shame and guilt and bringing long-standing issues to closure brings lightness to our life that was never present while we drank. It is not that we necessarily become persistently happy and bright, rather that we are no longer burdened by a huge weight of anguish.

But the damage caused by addiction isn't limited to horrific, shameful and guilty memories. Even when we have managed to stop drinking and remove what pain we can from our past then our mind still wants us to drink again. The memories underpinning all our triggers are that "drinking is good" and "drinking is fun"; and stopping drinking does not remove these. Drinking triggers lose their ferocity by denying them repeatedly over an extended period but the validations and justifications we constructed to support them still exist. "No-one will know", "You've done well, you deserve a drink", "Just one won't hurt", "Forever!" and "Poor me!" along with the idea that we are missing out on the fun in life are persistent thoughts that recur for years to come. They only cease to occur spontaneously when we regain fulfilling lives in the absence of alcohol. But achieving a worthwhile and fulfilling life means that we also have to live successfully in the community, and many have a severe deficiency in this respect.

One of the common features among alcoholics is that we never felt like we fitted in when we were young. Alcohol changed that for us and for many years to follow we drank at virtually every social occasion. One of the enduring consequences of addiction for many is that we are socially immature; we never learned to socialise sober as teenagers and as adults we drank to achieve social confidence. One of the great challenges in recovery is to overcome this. We have to learn how to socialise without alcohol, and we have to learn this from a position where we may have been deliberately distancing ourselves from social contact. At the same time as we feel an intense insecurity attending social functions we also know that they are almost certainly going to be triggering experiences. Learning to socialise again is a confusing amalgam of being uncomfortable among other people, fear of missing out, a vacuum of something uplifting occupying our days, and the danger of meeting powerful triggers. It is a difficult transition. For years or decades we have known exactly how our free time would be filled but now we have to re-join society as a non-drinker and find activities that constructively occupy the time we used to commit to drinking. Until we achieve this then we are condemned to resent our sobriety because we feel it steals our enjoyment of life and this resentment can be problematic as it occurs in a period of diminishing resolve. When we first stop drinking we do so because we have become desperate and this gives us heightened resolve. But as we extend our abstinence then this desperation fades because our distress lessens as the effects of alcohol-tolerance disappear. Our resolve diminishes as our distance from despair increases and this poses a great risk for those that are unhappy with their alcohol-free lives.

Relapse in this period is not uncommon. In the early stages of going without alcohol the effort is continuous and we have to be constantly vigilant and ready to fend off the cravings as they come. Relapse in this phase is often attributed to becoming "complacent", but that's not really what happens; what happens is that the problem changes and so does our perception of it. We no longer need to live on continuous high-alert because the constant onslaught of intense cravings has stopped. This coincides with our memories of just how desperate our life was while we drank being faded from recall. We stop building ourselves up for a daily battle and at the same time as the problem seems to have become less demanding our memory suggests that maybe we weren't that bad after all and we begin to doubt the necessity of stopping. While relapse is statistically far less likely in this phase than in the first few days and weeks it still happens and it often happens because desperation has been removed from our arsenal. But there is an odd occurrence in the months and years that follow that periodically reminds us of the importance of what we are doing, and these are drinking dreams. Relapse is a crushing event. It takes extraordinary strength to stand up again after a relapse and nobody experiencing one ever thinks that having that drink was worthwhile. Sooner or later everyone that relapses has to make another attempt at stopping drinking, but in one respect the experience of relapse gives them additional strength: it has been reinforced that stopping drinking is essential and drinking dreams do a similar thing. These dreams are incredibly vivid and in them we see ourselves drinking again, then as we start to emerge from the dream we become extremely alarmed that we *have* actually drunk again. It is incredibly shocking and for a few moments we experience what relapse would actually feel like.

Drinking dreams are a useful warning. They remind us that we are not "cured" and they remind us how awful we would feel if we did relapse.

Our sobriety begins as something incredibly fragile that can fracture at any moment but over time it becomes more resilient and robust. We don't suddenly change into a person that no longer drinks. Whether we like it or not our reward system still wants us to drink and it launches cravings to encourage that. Our mind still tells us what a good idea it is to have a drink, and our mind also tells us how much fun we are missing out on by not drinking. We have to keep fighting these ideas and that effort never truly ends; it diminishes in severity but it is always there in the background. The journey out of addiction is not a smooth or easy one. As we confront the cravings one by one then we slowly diminish their intensity, but we have so many triggers, and each trigger we deny summons a storm of mental justifications and lies. The effort seems to be without end, but it is not.

The timeline of recovery varies enormously from person to person. Those that have the characteristics favouring addiction more strongly and those that have drunk compulsively for longer have more to correct.

The physical recovery of the brain and body is guaranteed to happen in the absence of alcohol, but this happens at the body's own pace and each of us re-adapts at our own speed. The psychological recovery and social re-growth however are entirely up to the willingness of the individual to actively engage with them as issues and act to change them.

We don't particularly notice the moment when maintaining sobriety ceases to be a challenge, it's rather like we aren't aware of exactly when a headache stops hurting, but it is a wonderful day when we finally recognise it. However, even though we reach a point that we no longer display or feel any of the symptoms of addiction, we are not cured. There is no complete cure for alcoholism. While all the symptoms may disappear there are certain parts of the condition that remain. What has become known cannot become unknown and the mental pathways of addiction, while they may be un-traversed and dormant, still remain. In particular all of our drinking triggers still exit. They have lost their vigour but they are still present and there is no way to remove them completely. But the day comes that we suddenly realise that everything is different. We realise that we haven't noticed a significant craving for a while and we are for the most part calm and content. The "taut as a bowstring" stress is gone, the fear is gone, the constant demand to drink is gone, the hopelessness is gone and the incessant chatter in our head has subsided. The cravings still come from time to time, but the intensity has dropped to the point we can easily step past them as they occur. We still get the same old ideas coming in... "Just one would be nice!" but we can see them clearly as lies now and move on without being drawn into a mental debate. There is no miracle moment in recovery that marks the end, indeed there is no end; there are things we need to do and things we must not do for the rest of our lives. Recovery from addiction is a direction rather than a destination and there are disciplines we must maintain forever to keep ourselves well, but with practice they become simple to adhere to and require little of us on a day-to-day basis. When we reach this point we are not cured, but we *are* recovered.

If we drink again

Very few people manage to stop drinking at the first attempt, but even those that do had countless failed attempts at control before they made their first determined effort to stop. We try changing what we drink, where we drink, when we drink and how much we drink, and we try pausing for a while but nothing brings the problem under control. We are desperate to avoid the one guaranteed solution, to stop drinking altogether, because it is an unthinkable thought. Our biased memory insists that drinking is good and we can't imagine being without alcohol, it is the only "good" left in our lives. But after years of trying to contain our drinking we have to eventually give up on the idea that we can drink moderately; repeated and concerted efforts to do so have all failed. The defining difference between those that will succeed in an effort to stop drinking and those that can't yet is our understanding of this lack of control. Once we realise beyond all doubt that control is beyond us then it becomes possible to stop, but while we still hold even the smallest hope that we might one day re-gain control then this will cause our effort to fail sooner or later.

Success requires that we know with complete certainty that we cannot control our drinking and that we never will otherwise we are simply delaying the day that we *will* drink again. It is a huge step to reach and then sustain this position but drinking again is a certainty without it.

Eventually we take the plunge... drinking has to stop! Then and only then, when we actually try to stop permanently, do we start to recognise the true extent of our entrapment; until then we have only exposed a fraction of it. Many will fail to achieve lasting abstinence at the first attempt, some succeed after faltering once or twice and some fall into a prolonged pattern of stopping for a while then drinking, and stopping again. But if we *do* again drink then we re-invigorate drinking triggers.

The reward system is the engine that drives our drinking and it evolved to adapt to changing circumstances. A trigger strengthens when we act on it and secure the objective of the trigger, and it weakens when the trigger fails to secure the objective. In the wild a scenario where this would be advantageous is, for example, a fruit that is seasonal. After we have developed a trigger in response to the fruit being available we should change our behaviour when the fruit ceases to be in season otherwise we will waste a lot of time and energy searching for fruit that will never be found. So when we repeatedly fail to find the fruit where we anticipate it to be (because it is out of season) then the craving for it reduces in intensity. This is how denying cravings works. But there is another step of sophistication in the reward system that is described in the answer to this question: "What is the most successful behaviour when the fruit comes back into season?" The answer to this is that when the fruit comes back into season then the trigger should resume its full strength almost immediately, we should not waste time slowly working the trigger back up to strength. The trigger should recover its vigour as soon as the fruit becomes available again in order to gain the best advantage from the opportunity, and this is precisely how the reward system behaves. When the fruit comes back into season then the remnants of the trigger motivate us to approach and take the fruit. This reinforces the trigger, but now it does so very strongly indeed, and after only a few cycles of seeing and partaking of the fruit the trigger is restored to its full prior strength. Triggers may lose their strength through repeated failure but they are never forgotten because they may become helpful again at some time in the future and they regain their former strength very quickly once they start to be successful again. Unfortunately for us this is precisely what happens to all of our alcohol-related triggers. They are never forgotten and once we act on them again then their former strength is restored very quickly. Even after all the effort that goes into stripping triggers of their power we never manage to remove them completely; they sit there dormant, waiting to be reinvigorated.

It is perfectly common that alcoholics drink again after a period of being alcohol-free. There are many reasons we might do this but if often comes from the idea that we may now be able to control our drinking. This is an illusion but it is an appealing one and many are deceived by it. The deception is essentially that because we've managed to stop drinking then we have somehow proven that we can beat the problem. There are four changes that encourage this illusion; cravings lose their intensity, the effects of alcohol-tolerance reverse themselves out, the distance from despair means we no longer recall the intensity of how bad our life was, and the biased memory "drinking is good" continues to insist that we are missing out on fun now that we no longer drink. Many return to drinking in the mistaken belief that we will be able to control it this time, but this effort is doomed to fail sooner or later. For example, we might return to drinking in a controlled manner like only on a Friday after work. The first few times we may succeed in limiting our drinking like this, but on the occasions that we *do* drink we strongly reinvigorate the triggers relating to the circumstances. We strengthen triggers relating to the time, to the particular location and to certain people, but we also strengthen some universal triggers: the sight of alcohol and the smell of alcohol. This strengthens craving for alcohol not just on the Friday evening we gave ourselves permission to drink, but also any time we smell or see (or see in pictures or imagine) alcohol. Each Friday we strengthen these triggers further and soon the strengthened cravings and accompanying mental justifications lead us to drink outside of the boundary we imposed on ourselves. Unless we intervene to halt this process then we reinvigorate more and more triggers and soon find ourselves drinking exactly like we did before.

Trying to return to drinking in a controlled manner may appear to work for a limited period but unless it is interrupted it will always re-escalate beyond our control. If we return to drinking *without* placing any boundaries or limits on ourselves then we will bring all our main drinking triggers back up to their former strength alarmingly quickly: in just a few days. But reinvigorating our drinking triggers is not the only consequence of relapse, something else happens that is equally serious.

The reward system evolved to respond to changing circumstances and so did the brain; it changes the way it works to optimally maintain its speed and efficiency. While we drank heavily then our brain adapted to regular alcohol impairment by accelerating processing speed, elevating the flight-or-fight response, and by lowering serotonin and dopamine release. All of these adaptations reverse back to normal levels once we are alcohol-free again for a period. But when our brain function is once again impaired by regular and high blood/alcohol levels then our brain recognises that it has met these conditions before and it reinstates all the remedial measures that were effective previously. When we resume drinking heavily and regularly then all of the changes that our brain made when becoming alcohol-tolerant are put back in place; our mood is lowered by reduced serotonin release, our brain speed is increased by increased glutamate release and decreased GABA release, and our flight-or-fight response is heightened by increased cortisol, adrenaline and noradrenaline levels. But this doesn't take the months or years that it took the first time, this happens within days. Within a very short time-span we are thrown right back to the same state of fear, anxiety, restlessness and hopelessness that had previously taken years to accumulate. When this happens we once again become locked into the feedback loop of drinking to relieve the symptoms of drinking and our spiral down into hopelessness returns. Resuming regular drinking commits this reversal but crucially taking a few drinks does not. Yes, any drinking at all will reinvigorate some triggers, but if we have the presence of mind to intervene and stop quickly then no further damage is done. Most significantly, if we only have a few drinks and then stop then we *do not* cause the brain to re-implement all the defensive measures engaged to fend off the consequences of being regularly alcohol-impaired: it does not re-instate the measures taken that come with alcohol-tolerance. This also means that we do not re-activate the feedback loop of addiction where we drink to relieve our distress.

It is not inevitable that if we drink again we will end up in exactly the same position as we started, not at all. If we limit that drinking to a single, or very few drinks then the only significant damage is to our self-esteem. If however we drink repeatedly and heavily then we recommit all the brain-altering effects of alcohol-tolerance and the effect on our self-image can be completely crushing.

The emotional consequences of relapse can be extremely severe. The earlier failures, drinking more or more often than we intended, are frustrating and confusing but drinking again after a period of abstinence can be utterly devastating. It feels like complete and total failure; we have failed in front of those close to us, we have failed in front of our peers, and we have failed ourselves. All we had to do was one simple thing, something that everyone else in the world seems able to do quite easily... but somehow we cannot do it and the position seems to be more hopeless than ever. The earlier sense of impending doom and hopelessness returns in full force and this is deepened by the new evidence that for us it really *is* impossible to stop drinking. Not only have we failed ourselves we have failed everyone else and it seems that we really *are* the hopeless alcoholic that everyone says. It is a complete collapse of self-worth. Relapse feels terrible, like complete failure, but it really shouldn't be seen like this. It seems like we are back at the beginning, but even if the relapse led to a significant period of heavy drinking then we are still nothing like back at the beginning: we still know what we learned, and we have learned a lot.

Learning to be alcohol-free is very like learning to ride a bicycle. The first challenge is to manage staying upright while making forward progress. How many times did we fall before achieving that? But once we'd learned how to maintain balance and move in the direction we wanted there were still many occasions when we fell... because the problem had changed. Yes, we knew how to keep balance, but sometimes we grew over-confident, and sometimes something unforeseen would happen and we'd be down on the ground again. Stopping drinking is a learning challenge that is very much like this; it changes. When we first try to curb our drinking the cravings, those wordless demands that we drink, catch us time after time. Eventually we learn to confront and overcome the cravings and manage to string a few wobbly days together. Then we gather speed and confidence and set off careering down the sober road, but that's not where the learning story ends. Once we learned to balance on a bike the challenge became different. It no longer took all our concentration to stay upright: we'd mastered balance. The challenges now were overconfidence and the unexpected; we'd try to go too fast, or something unforeseen happened like suddenly hitting a slippery patch while cornering. These are just like the challenges we meet when we've achieved a sober period; we become over confident ("perhaps I'm cured", "I can manage just one" etc.) or we fail to negotiate something that was sudden and unexpected (out-of-the-blue cravings). When we first get sober the challenge is relentless... it requires continuous and determined effort, but once past this the challenges become intermittent. As we close the pathways in our mind to alcohol one-by-one our addiction searches for pathways that are still open and tests us from a new direction. The problem changes and we have to learn to meet the new challenges as they come.

We don't just get one chance at learning to ride a bike and if we did then nobody would ever succeed. When we fell it wasn't because we chose to, it was because we lacked the expertise not to. We had to fall in order to learn, and stopping drinking sometimes requires similar learning. We often count days since we last drank as the measurement of success but it is important to recognise just what this is, or more importantly, what it is not. The number of sober days we have accumulated only means the number of consecutive days of abstinence and this is not a measure of recovery, it is a measure of sobriety. Recovery is not determined by the length of time since our last drink but by our mental wellness, and the two can be quite independent of each other. If we drink again then our length of continuous sobriety is lost but our recovery isn't. We don't only get one go at stopping drinking, we get as many as it takes, and relapse is not the end of a recovery effort; it is only a pause along the path. We don't have to go right back to the beginning and start the process all over again. When we fell off the bike we weren't put back at the start of learning how to ride, we are exactly as far advanced along that path as we were when we fell. Nothing was lost other that a bit of pride and skin. Everything that had been learned was still learned, and because of this fall we will do better at our next attempt. Relapse while trying to stop drinking is precisely like this; we are not put back at the start of recovery. We still know everything that we have learned thus far and we just learned something new. A relapse does not put us back at the beginning of our recovery. In fact, as long as we learn from the event, it advances us.

Stopping drinking is difficult and we don't fully understand how hard it is until we begin in earnest. As we start out we are completely unaware of the full ferocity of cravings or all the ways that our minds will try to trick us into drinking again, we only discover these as we advance. Sometimes they will catch us out and we drink. But relapse isn't failure it is education. If we relapse then it is a necessary learning step on the path to recovery. A relapse hasn't made the problem worse, the problem is unchanged. We are still an alcoholic, we still can't limit or control our drinking, and drinking will drive us into a downward spiral of despair. What *has* changed though is our ability to overcome it.

If we only got one attempt at learning to ride a bicycle then nobody in the world would be able to do it... yet millions can. Similarly, nobody ever said we only get one chance at getting sober; we don't, we get as many as it takes. Nobody, absolutely nobody is able to completely stop drinking at the first attempt, it is always preceded by relapse in one form or another; failures to limit the amount we drink, drinking on occasions we intended not to, or failing to not drink for a set period of time. We don't need to have some rare super-power to stop drinking. What we need is to learn from our mistakes and the will to try again.

Regardless of how long we remain sober we are never completely free from the possibility of relapse and recovery from alcoholism should be regarded as bringing the condition into remission rather than removing it completely. If we ever think that we have beaten addiction and can have "just one" then we will soon discover to our dismay that our drinking is again completely beyond our control. We can stop drinking and alter our condition so that it no longer interferes with our lives but we can't remove our addiction completely; those drinking triggers are still there and they always will be. In this respect we are never completely cured because the roots of alcoholism remain in the reward system forever.

If we ever drink regularly again then we very quickly re-invigorate the triggers we acted on, and if we continue to drink then alcohol-tolerance will re-establish itself and we will soon find ourselves exactly back where we were. This is not something that sometimes happens it is something that *always* happens. This is how the reward system works, it is how our brain attempts to protect itself and we cannot prevent it from happening. There are no exceptions to this. Nobody, has *ever* become a normal drinker after being an alcoholic. If you are an alcoholic, still drinking or in recovery, then this is one of the most important things you can know: alcoholics can *never* drink moderately again. There are no exceptions to this and you will not be the first.

The Last Words

Society tells us that alcoholics are weak and worthless and that we wouldn't be in this position if we only exercised more control over ourselves. But this book has described how that control is taken from us. It is taken without our involvement, it is taken without our permission, and we didn't even know it was happening. Alcoholism is not poor control, poor morals, or weakness and it is not shameful, yet this is what society tells us. The very thought of being an alcoholic is so loaded with shame and failure that we dare not acknowledge the truth of our position, even to ourselves. But the picture society paints is completely incorrect. We do not drink because we are weak and should control ourselves better, we do so because our brain urges us to drink extremely strongly and only rarely motivates against it. But normal drinkers are motivated to drink and to avoid drink in equal measure, and they judge us by that experience.

With respect to alcohol there are four main ways that our brains behave differently to those of regular drinkers.

#1 Our reward system responds differently to alcohol. Our brain greatly values the advantages of drinking over the disadvantages. This causes us to develop a huge number of powerful drinking triggers, but we only create a very few drink-avoiding triggers.

#2 Our memory remembers "do this again" every time we drink significantly and this is reinforced by dopamine but it actively fades the memories of drinking occasions that had a bad outcome. This leads to our recall of alcohol being overwhelmingly positive and the downsides of alcohol are grossly undervalued.

#3 Heightened motivation to drink coming from the reward system makes us drink regularly and heavily over an extended period and our brain changes how it works to compensate for regular alcohol impairment. When we are sober these changes cause us to be anxious, miserable, fearful, agitated, and alone with a sense of impending doom. We develop powerful drinking triggers associated with the negative emotions caused by prolonged and heavy drinking and these triggers are fired whenever we are sober.

#4 Our brain recognises and moves to resolve the conflict between drinking being a good thing (verified by our memory) and a bad thing (supported by direct evidence of bad things happening and what other people tell us). Our brain finds that "drinking is good" is the better supported argument and creates justifications that uphold this position: our brain actively encourages continued drinking.

The unbalanced reward system and the changes that come with alcohol-tolerance lock us into a self-reinforcing feedback loop whereby alcohol-tolerance brings on adverse emotional changes which are relieved by drinking... and these in turn further strengthen the drinking triggers. Any desire or willingness to change our drinking patterns is opposed by our biased memory and the psychological justifications that support why we should continue to drink. These four components trap us in a vicious cycle down into anxiety, fear, depression and hopelessness that left unchecked will kill us.

None of this is chosen. These four components of addiction form, operate, and strengthen entirely automatically and we have no direct or immediate control over any of them. When society tells us that we are making bad choices and exercising poor control they do so from their own viewpoint; they *have* that freedom of choice, but we do not. For us the choice to drink is made automatically, it is supported by memories that assure us that drinking is a good thing and arguments in our head tell us that drinking now is a good idea; it will make us feel better, we deserve it, everybody does it, and so on. For us to *not* drink we have to notice and then contradict our own mind's automatically generated instruction to drink, and we have to do this while our mind insists that drinking is a perfectly reasonable course of action. This is difficult to do once, it is very difficult to do many times in a row, and it is extremely difficult to do day-in, day-out. But to gain lasting freedom from alcohol we don't just have to do this once, we have to do it many times a day, day after day, over a protracted period, and we must be successful *every single time* because a single failure will result in relapse. We have to maintain our clarity of purpose even as increasing distance from despair makes the pain of continued drinking fade, and we have to maintain resolve even though the challenge seems never ending. This is what is required to free ourselves from addiction.

This book describes the mechanisms of addiction, but this is far more than just interesting information. This knowledge has direct application for three groups of people in particular; those diagnosing the problem, those assisting in recovery, and alcoholics themselves.

The greatest barrier to overcome in recovery is denial; before this is broken there is no pathway to recovery at all and people in primary healthcare can have a large role in challenging denial. General Practitioners are particularly important in this regard as they are seen as authority figures and their words carry more weight than those of our families or peers. Few alcoholics will present themselves seeking advice for dealing with addiction... it is a shameful thing that we don't want to share even in the confidentiality of a doctor's office. If alcoholics visit their doctor at all for this problem then most will seek help for stress or depression. Medication may help those in distress for other reasons but will not help alcoholics in whom the depression is *caused* by drinking... it may even exacerbate the problem. This gives doctors a dilemma: is the patient suffering this depression because they have become alcohol-tolerant or for other reasons? There is a simple way to test for this. One of the four components of addiction is a heavily biased memory, the unshakable knowledge that drinking is fun and good, and this is not present in those who are suffering stress or depression for other reasons. Addiction as a cause of the distress can be exposed by telling the patient that there is medication that will help, but they mustn't drink for the whole time they take it... and pay close attention to the reaction. If the reaction is instant shock, confusion and fear then this strongly indicates alcoholism because this is not the reaction of someone whose drinking is not compulsive. Alcoholics typically believe that their experience is unique to them. But when an authority figure presents the various ways that addiction manifests itself, ways that even the sufferer themselves has not yet connected then this is a serious challenge to their denial. Even if this does not immediately lead to the sufferer addressing their addiction it may bring forward the day that they do... and this is a major win.

This book is also written for those directly helping others break free from addiction. Alcoholism is a complex condition that alters our behaviour, memory, emotions and thoughts and we struggle to make sense of what is happening to us. We don't only struggle with this while we are still drinking we continue to struggle when we stop. We also have difficulty reconciling the actions we are encouraged to take in recovery with what we perceive to be the problem. We are encouraged to do many things in recovery and often the purpose of many of these is not immediately apparent. This book helps counsellors, peer support workers and sponsors explain what part of the problem each recommended action addresses. It allows them to explain what facet of addiction each remedial action is directed at and how it will help.

The last and main audience for this book is alcoholics ourselves. People can give us advice until they are blue in the face but we will dismiss it until we believe that the action they recommend is warranted. We resist doing things we don't like until we believe they are necessary and understand how they will help us. Nobody else can do what is required to achieve and maintain recovery; we have to do it ourselves... and this requires conviction. While we believe that our problem is down to not trying hard enough to control our behaviour then we focus on precisely that... trying harder. But when we recognise that we don't drink because we apply poor control, we drink because our brain demands that we do so, then we begin to focus on addressing the real problem which is the destructive way in which our mind is working.

The primary aim of this book is to shatter denial. If you are alcoholic then you will have recognised your condition in the pages of this book and you will now understand that progression of the condition is inevitable: it will get worse if it is not stopped. You are also now able to separate the aspects of your daily experience that are products of the condition from those that are the products of your circumstances and you can see the full reach of the condition into your existence. But this book not only shows how far reaching are the consequences of alcoholism; it also shows which aspects of our thinking are problematic and require correction.

Stopping drinking is not the challenge it appears to be. Our fight is not with the bottle but with ourselves and when we understand all the ways in which our brain is trying to make us drink then we can be objective in how we confront it. This book takes the mystery out of addiction and the guesswork out of recovery.

There is no magic pill or potion we can take that will cure alcoholism and there is no easy route out of addiction. But if we do not find a way out then the condition is fatal. We also cannot simply sit and hope for it to disappear, it will not, it will get worse. Recovery is not a passive process. Our minds are working in ways that will destroy us and we have to change how they work or we will die, it really is that simple. But nothing changes if nothing changes. We have to *do* things that alter how we think and we have to do them despite what our mind is telling us. This book lays out in detail the problems to be addressed and this in turn allows us to focus effort where it will yield results. But knowledge alone is not enough, we must then apply it. We cannot *want* ourselves into recovery, we have to *act*.

If you do not change direction you will probably end up where you are headed.

Lao Tzu

Additional reading

The information in this book is based on insights into alcoholism provided by current science and research. Below are some of the research papers detailing the science behind the main themes of the content.

Definition, descriptions and symptoms

The American Medical Association

- Morse RM, Flavin DK. The Definition of Alcoholism. JAMA. 1992;268(8):1012–1014. doi:10.1001/jama.1992.03490080086030

The American Psychiatric Association

- American Psychiatric Association. (2013). Diagnostic and statistical manual of mental disorders (5th ed.). Washington, DC: See "Substance-related disorders", sub-section "Alcohol use disorder"

The World Health Organisation

- ICD-10 Classifications of Mental and Behavioural Disorder: Clinical Descriptions and Diagnostic Guidelines. Geneva. World Health Organisation. 1992. See Section F10. – "Mental and behavioural disorders due to use of alcohol"

The risks and damage attributable to alcohol

- GBD 2016 Alcohol Collaborators. Alcohol use and burden for 195 countries and territories, 1990-2016: a systematic analysis for the Global Burden of Disease Study 2016. Lancet. 2018 Sep 22;392(10152):1015-1035. doi: 10.1016/S0140-6736(18)31310-2.

- Global status report on alcohol and health 2018. Geneva: World Health Organization; 2018. Licence: CC BY-NC-SA 3.0 IGO

- Shield, Kevin D et al. Chronic diseases and conditions related to alcohol use. Alcohol research : current reviews vol. 35,2 (2014): 155-73

- Rehm, J., and Shield, K. Alcohol and mortality: Global alcohol-attributable deaths from cancer, liver cirrhosis, and injury in 2010. Alcohol Research: Current Reviews 35(2):174–183, 2013. PMID: 24881325

The dopamine reward and aversion system

- Schultz, Wolfram. Neuronal Reward and Decision Signals: From Theories to Data. Physiological reviews vol. 95,3 (2015): 853-951

- Fischer, Adrian G and Markus Ullsperger. An Update on the Role of Serotonin and its Interplay with Dopamine for Reward. Frontiers in human neuroscience vol. 11 484. 11 Oct. 2017, doi:10.3389/fnhum.2017.00484

- Hailan Hu; Reward and Aversion, Annual Review of Neuroscience 2016 39:1, 297-324

Neurotransmitters (Dopamine, Serotonin, GABA glutamate) and alcoholism

- Clapp P, Bhave SV, Hoffman PL. How adaptation of the brain to alcohol leads to dependence: a pharmacological perspective. Alcohol Res Health. 2008;31(4):310-39. Review. PubMed PMID: 20729980; PubMed Central PMCID: PMC2923844

- Banerjee, Niladri. Neurotransmitters in alcoholism: A review of neurobiological and genetic studies. Indian journal of human genetics vol. 20,1 (2014): 20-31

- Chastain G. Alcohol, neurotransmitter systems, and behavior. J Gen Psychol 2006 Oct;133(4):329-35. Review. PubMed PMID: 17128954

- Clapp, Peter et al. How adaptation of the brain to alcohol leads to dependence: a pharmacological perspective; Alcohol research & health : the journal of the National Institute on Alcohol Abuse and Alcoholism vol. 31,4 (2008): 310-39

- Volkow ND, Wiers CE, Shokri-Kojori E, Tomasi D, Wang GJ, Baler R; Neurochemical and metabolic effects of acute and chronic alcohol in the human brain: Studies with positron emission tomography; Neuropharmacology. 2017 Aug 1;122:175-188

- Cloninger CR. Neurogenetic adaptive mechanisms in alcoholism. Science. 1987 Apr 24;236(4800):410-6. PubMed PMID: 2882604

- Gerald A. Deehan, Christopher P. Knight, R. Aaron Waeiss, Eric A. Engleman, Jamie E. Toalston, William J. McBride, Sheketha R. Hauser, Zachary A. Rodd;

Peripheral Administration of Ethanol Results in a Correlated Increase in Dopamine and Serotonin Within the Posterior Ventral Tegmental Area, Alcohol and Alcoholism, Volume 51, Issue 5, 1 September 2016, Pages 535–540

- Fernando Valenzuela, C. (1997). Alcohol and Neurotransmitter Interactions. Alcohol Health Res World. 2. 144-148

Reduced recognition of adverse effects

- Cacciaglia R, Nees F, Pohlack ST, Ruttorf M, Winkelmann T, Witt SH, Nieratschker V, Rietschel M, Flor H. A risk variant for alcoholism in the NMDA receptor affects amygdala activity during fear conditioning in humans. Biol Psychol. 2013 Sep;94(1):74-81. doi: 10.1016/j.biopsycho.2013.05.006.

- Finn PR, Mazas CA, Justus AN, Steinmetz J. Early-onset alcoholism with conduct disorder: go/no go learning deficits, working memory capacity, and personality. Alcohol Clin Exp Res. 2002 Feb;26(2):186-206. PubMed PMID: 11964558.

- Trick, Leanne et al. Impaired fear recognition and attentional set-shifting is associated with brain structural changes in alcoholic patients: Addiction biology vol. 19,6 (2014): 1041-54.

Dopamine and alcoholism

- Ma, Hui and Gang Zhu. The dopamine system and alcohol dependence. Shanghai archives of psychiatry vol. 26,2 (2014): 61-8

- Bustamante, Diego et al; Ethanol induces stronger dopamine release in nucleus accumbens (shell) of alcohol-preferring (bibulous) than in alcohol-avoiding (abstainer) rats; European journal of pharmacology vol. 591,1-3 (2008): 153-8

- Volkow ND, Tomasi D, Wang GJ, Telang F, Fowler JS, Logan J, Maynard LJ, Wong CT. Predominance of D2 receptors in mediating dopamine's effects in brain metabolism: effects of alcoholism. J Neurosci. 2013 Mar 6;33(10):4527-35. doi: 10.1523/JNEUROSCI.5261-12.2013

- Hirth N, Meinhardt MW, Noori HR, Salgado H, Torres-Ramirez O, Uhrig S, Broccoli L, Vengeliene V, Roßmanith M, Perreau-Lenz S, Köhr G, Sommer WH, Spanagel R, Hansson AC. Convergent evidence from alcohol-dependent humans and rats for a hyperdopaminergic state in protracted abstinence. Proc Natl Acad Sci US A. 2016 Mar 15;113(11):3024-9

- Hansson AC, Gründer G, Hirth N, Noori HR, Spanagel R, Sommer WH; Dopamine and opioid systems adaptation in alcoholism revisited: Convergent evidence from positron emission tomography and postmortem studies; Neurosci Biobehav Rev. 2018 Sep 19. pii: S0149-7634(18)30110-6

Serotonin and alcoholism

- Nishikawa M, Diksic M, Sakai Y, Kumano H, Charney D, Palacios-Boix J, Negrete J, Gill K. Alterations in brain serotonin synthesis in male alcoholics measured using positron emission tomography. Alcohol Clin Exp Res. 2009 Feb;33(2):233-9

- Underwood, Mark D et al. Serotonin receptors and suicide, major depression, alcohol use disorder and reported early life adversity. Translational psychiatry vol. 8,1 279. 14 Dec. 2018, doi:10.1038/s41398-018-0309-1

- Christopher J. Morgan, Abdulla A.-B. Badawy; Alcohol-induced euphoria: exclusion of serotonin, Alcohol and Alcoholism, Volume 36, Issue 1, 1 January 2001, Pages 22–25

- Sari, Youssef et al. Role of the serotonergic system in alcohol dependence: from animal models to clinics. Progress in molecular biology and translational science vol. 98 (2011): 401-43

GABA and alcoholism

- Enoch, Mary-Anne. The role of GABA(A) receptors in the development of alcoholism. Pharmacology, biochemistry, and behavior vol. 90,1 (2008): 95-104

- Olsen, Richard W and Jing Liang. Role of GABAA receptors in alcohol use disorders suggested by chronic intermittent ethanol (CIE) rodent model. Molecular brain vol. 10, 1 45. 20 Sep. 2017, doi:10.1186/s13041-017-0325-8

Glutamate and alcoholism

- Alasmari F, Goodwani S, McCullumsmith RE, Sari Y; Role of glutamatergic system and mesocorticolimbic circuits in alcohol dependence; Prog Neurobiol. 2018 Dec;171:32-49

- Gonzales, Rueben A., and Jason N. Jaworski. Alcohol and glutamate. Alcohol Health & Research World, Spring 1997, p. 120+

Cortisol, adrenaline, norepinephrine and alcoholism

- Lovallo, William R. Cortisol secretion patterns in addiction and addiction risk. International journal of psychophysiology : official journal of the International Organization of Psychophysiology vol. 59,3 (2006): 195-202

- Badrick, Ellena et al. The relationship between alcohol consumption and cortisol secretion in an aging cohort. Journal of clinical endocrinology and metabolism vol. 93,3 (2007): 750-7

- Stein, Michael D and Peter D Friedmann. Disturbed sleep and its relationship to alcohol use. Substance abuse vol. 26,1 (2005): 1-13

Alcohol and memory

- White, A. M. (2003). What Happened? Alcohol, Memory Blackouts, and the Brain. Alcohol Research & Health, 27(2), 186-196

- Petruccelli, Feyder, Ledru, Jaques, Anderson, Kaun; Alcohol Activates Scabrous-Notch to Influence Associated Memories; Neuron. 2018 Dec 5;100(5):1209-1223.e4

Distress and addiction

- Newman EL, Leonard MZ, Arena DT, de Almeida RMM, Miczek KA; Social defeat stress and escalation of cocaine and alcohol consumption: Focus on CRF; Neurobiol Stress. 2018 Sep 19;9:151-165

- Sinha, Rajita. Chronic stress, drug use, and vulnerability to addiction Annals of the New York Academy of Sciences vol. 1141 (2008): 105-30

- George DT, Nutt DJ, Dwyer BA, Linnoila M. Alcoholism and panic disorder: is the comorbidity more than coincidence? Acta Psychiatr Scand. 1990 Feb;81(2):97-107. Review. PubMed PMID: 2183544

Cravings

- Heinz, Andreas & Loeber, Sabine & Georgi, Alexander & Wrase, Jana & Hermann, Derik & Rey, Eibe-R & Wellek, Stefan & Mann, Karl. (2003). REWARD CRAVING AND WITHDRAWAL RELIEF CRAVING: ASSESSMENT OF DIFFERENT MOTIVATIONAL PATHWAYS TO ALCOHOL INTAKE. Alcohol and alcoholism (Oxford, Oxfordshire). 38. 35-9. 10.1093/alcalc/agg005

- Grüsser SM, Mörsen CP, Flor H. Alcohol craving in problem and occasional alcohol drinkers. Alcohol Alcohol. 2006 Jul-Aug;41(4):421-5. Epub 2006 Apr 24. PubMed PMID: 16636008

- Johnson, Brian. Addiction and will. Frontiers in human neuroscience vol. 7 545. 11 Sep. 2013, doi:10.3389/fnhum.2013.00545

Psychological impacts of alcoholism

- M Wierońska, Joanna & Stachowicz, K & Nowak, Gabriel & Pilc, Andrzej. (2011). The Loss of Glutamate-GABA

Harmony in Anxiety Disorders. INTECH Open Access Publisher, 2011. ISBN 9533075929 & 9789533075921

- Goleman, Daniel. 1995. Emotional intelligence: why it can matter more than IQ. New York: Bantam Books.

- Boschloo, L., Vogelzangs, N., Van den Brink, W., Smit, J., Veltman, D., Beekman, A., & Penninx, B. (2012). Alcohol use disorders and the course of depressive and anxiety disorders. British Journal of Psychiatry, 200(6), 476-484. doi:10.1192/bjp.bp.111.097550

- Tollefson GD. Anxiety and alcoholism: a serotonin link. Br J Psychiatry Suppl. 1991 Sep;(12):34-9. Review. PubMed PMID: 1840761

- Thorberg FA, Lyvers M. Attachment, fear of intimacy and differentiation of self among clients in substance disorder treatment facilities. Addict Behav. 2006 Apr;31(4):732-7. Epub 2005 Jun 20. PubMed PMID: 15970395

- Głogowska, Karolina & Wyrzykowska, Ewa & Mickiewicz, Kinga. (2014). Attachment relationships among people addicted to alcohol. Alcoholism & Drug Addiction. 27. 145-161

- Charles Kornreich, Pierre Philippot, Marie-Line Foisy, Sylvie Blairy, Emmanuel Raynaud, Bernard Dan, Ursula Hess, Xavier Noël, Isy Pelc, Paul Verbanck; Impaired emotional facial expression recognition is associated with interpersonal problems in alcoholism, Alcohol and Alcoholism, Volume 37, Issue 4, 1 July 2002, Pages 394-400

- Sadava, S. W., & Thompson, M. M. (1986). Loneliness, social drinking, and vulnerability to alcohol problems. Canadian Journal of Behavioural Science / Revue canadienne des sciences du comportement, 18(2), 133-139

- Winokur, G. (1983). Alcoholism and depression. Substance & Alcohol Actions/Misuse, 4(2-3), 111-119.

- Brière, Frédéric N et al. Comorbidity between major depression and alcohol use disorder from adolescence to adulthood. Comprehensive psychiatry vol. 55,3 (2013): 526-33

- Waska R. Addictions and the quest to control the object. Am J Psychoanal. 2006 Mar;66(1):43-62. PubMed PMID: 16544198

- Kendall RE. Alcohol and suicide. Subst Alcohol Actions Misuse. 1983;4(2-3):121-7. PubMed PMID: 6648755

Genetics and inheritability

- Whitlock, F., Price, J., & Weston, M. (1978). Inheritance of Alcoholism. British Journal of Psychiatry, 133(3), 286-286. doi:10.1192/bjp.133.3.286

- Edenberg, Howard J and Tatiana Foroud. "Genetics and alcoholism" Nature reviews. Gastroenterology & hepatology vol. 10,8 (2013): 487-94

- Saraswat, Smriti. (2016). Genetic Predisposition to Alcoholism. Journal of Public Health and Allied Sciences. Volume I. 5

- Foley PF, Loh EW, Innes DJ, Williams SM, Tannenberg AE, Harper CG, Dodd PR. Association studies of neurotransmitter gene polymorphisms in alcoholic Caucasians. Ann N Y Acad Sci. 2004 Oct;1025:39-46. PubMed PMID: 15542698

Susceptibility to alcoholism

- Slutske WS, Heath AC, Madden PA, Bucholz KK, Statham DJ, Martin NG. Personality and the genetic risk for alcohol dependence. J Abnorm Psychol. 2002 Feb;111(1):124-33. PubMed PMID: 11871377

- Littlefield AK, Stevens AK, Sher KJ. Impulsivity and Alcohol Involvement: Multiple, Distinct Constructs and Processes. Curr Addict Rep. 2014 Mar;1(1):33-40. doi: 10.1007/s40429-013-0004-5

- Al Birţ, M & Şandor, V & Vaida, Aura & Birţ, M.E.. (2008). Alexithymia, a risk factor in alcohol addiction? A brief research report on Romanian population. Journal of Cognitive and Behavioral Psychotherapies. 8. 217-225.

Addiction Transference

- DiFranza JR, Guerrera MP. Alcoholism and smoking. J Stud Alcohol. 1990 Mar;51(2):130-5

Dopamine, Serotonin, and Norepinephrine at and after withdrawal

- Patkar AA, Gopalakrishnan R, Naik PC, Murray HW, Vergare MJ, Marsden CA. Changes in plasma noradrenaline and serotonin levels and craving during alcohol withdrawal. Alcohol. 2003 May-Jun;38(3):224-31. PubMed PMID: 12711656

- Hirth, Natalie & Meinhardt, Marcus & Noori, Hamid & Salgado, Humberto & Torres-Ramirez, Oswaldo & Uhrig,

195

Stefanie & Broccoli, Laura & Vengeliene, Valentina & Roßmanith, Martin & Perreau, Stéphanie & Köhr, Georg & Sommer, Wolfgang & Spanagel, Rainer & Hansson, Anita. (2016). Convergent evidence from alcohol-dependent humans and rats for a hyperdopaminergic state in protracted abstinence. Proceedings of the National Academy of Sciences. 113. 10.1073/pnas.1506012113

- Laine TP, Ahonen A, Torniainen P, Heikkilä J, Pyhtinen J, Räsänen P, Niemelä O, Hillbom M. Dopamine transporters increase in human brain after alcohol withdrawal. Mol Psychiatry. 1999 Mar;4(2):189-91, 104-5. PubMed PMID: 10208452

Made in the USA
Las Vegas, NV
05 January 2021